CLASS OF
'37

Hester Barron is Senior Lecturer in History at the University of Sussex. She teaches and writes about working-class life, childhood, schooling and education. Her first book, *The 1926 Miners' Lockout*, is a history of the coalfield communities of Durham, where she grew up. She now lives in the South Downs.

Claire Langhamer is Director of the Institute of Historical Research, University of London, and a Trustee of the Mass Observation Archive. Her work is about ordinary people's feelings and experiences; her books include *The English in Love*. She grew up in Yorkshire, studied in Lancashire and now lives in Brighton.

HESTER BARRON & CLAIRE LANGHAMER

CLASS OF '37

Voices from working-class girlhood

metro

Published by Metro Publishing,
an imprint of Bonnier Books UK
4th Floor, Victoria House,
Bloomsbury Square,
London WC1B 4DA
Owned by Bonnier Books
Sveavägen 56, Stockholm, Sweden

www.facebook.com/johnblakebooks
twitter.com/jblakebooks

Paperback: 978-1-78946-408-5
Hardback: 978-1-78946-405-4
Ebook: 978-1-78946-460-1
Audio: 978-1-78946-407-8

Design by www.envydesign.co.uk

Printed and bound in Great Britain by Clays Ltd, Elcograf S.p.A

1 3 5 7 9 10 8 6 4 2

Text copyright © Hester Barron and Claire Langhamer 2021

The right of Hester Barron and Claire Langhamer to be identified as the authors
of this work has been asserted by them in accordance with the Copyright,
Designs and Patents Act 1988.

Map by Liane Payne, based on 1939 Ordnance Survey map reproduced with the
permission of the National Library of Scotland

Metro Publishing is an imprint of Bonnier Books UK
www.bonnierbooks.co.uk

For Idris and Izzy
Who are also growing up in an uncertain world
but who make it a better place

Contents

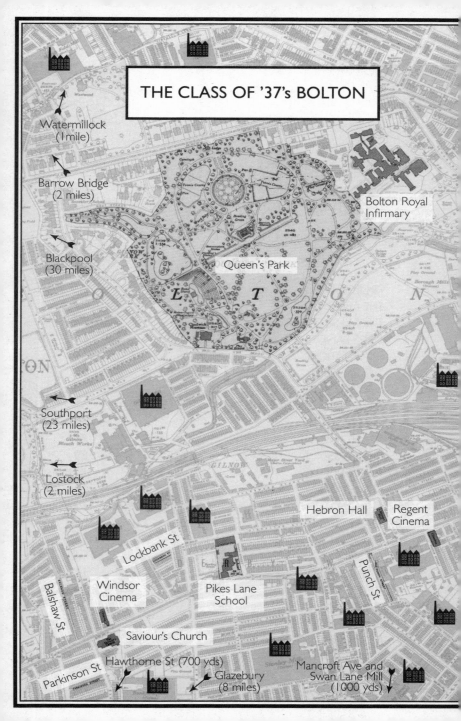

THE CLASS OF '37's BOLTON

Watermillock
(1 mile)

Barrow Bridge
(2 miles)

Blackpool
(30 miles)

Bolton Royal
Infirmary

Queen's Park

Southport
(23 miles)

Lostock
(2 miles)

Hebron Hall

Regent
Cinema

Lockbank St

Punch St

Windsor
Cinema

Pikes Lane
School

Balshaw St

Saviour's Church

Parkinson St

Hawthorne St (700 yds)

Glazebury
(8 miles)

Mancroft Ave and
Swan Lane Mill
(1000 yds)

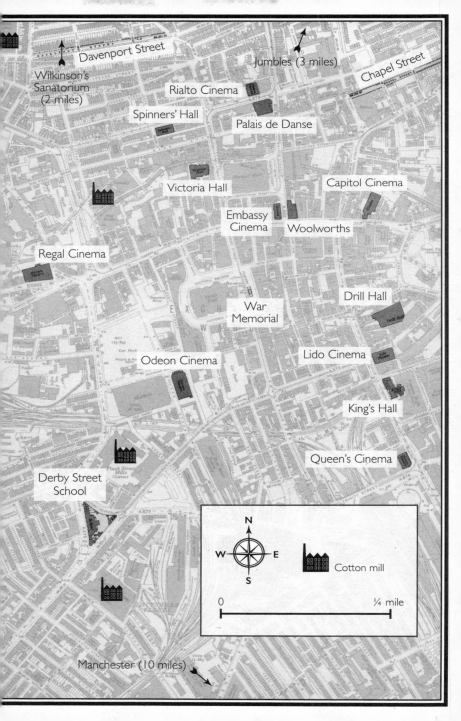

Prologue

A twelve-year-old girl chews the end of her pen, deep in thought. Her teacher has asked what she would like to be when she grows up, though she is a couple of years away yet from leaving school. 'I think I should like to keep a shop,' she decides, after some moments, and in a neat, curling script she sets down her thoughts:

> I should like to be able to keep a shop as I like serving the little boys and girls with sweets. The women would buy loaves which I could tie up in a parcel. But for this work you must be honest. In some shops where there are valuable goods, they test you by putting a two shilling piece and if you are honest you give it back and you get the job. But if you are not honest you think they have lost it and you keep it and are sacked.

It is May 1937, and the girl is a schoolchild in the Lancashire mill town of Bolton. Over the next few months, she and her classmates will write several essays about the world as they see it and the things that matter to them – about their homes and how they spend their time, about the royal family, about the cinema, about Heaven, about their dreams. Their mothers might have had few choices when they had left school aged twelve, but these girls want to be actresses, authors, seamstresses and chemists. Not for them the cotton mills, they think.

There is no premonition in the girls' writings about the conflict that is soon to come. As they sit in their classroom and thoughtfully set out their hopes for the future, the Basque town of Guernica smoulders following the devastating attack by German and Italian bombers. In London and Berlin, rearmament programmes are being cranked up. In Whitehall, mandarins are quietly making plans for the evacuation of children out of British cities should terrifying predictions of mass aerial bombardment come to pass. By the end of the year, Japan and China will already be at war.

The classmates will grow into young women against the backdrop of war. They will conduct their first courtships in blacked-out streets and grieve for boyfriends and brothers conscripted abroad. They will join the ranks of women mobilised into war service in the new munitions, shell-filling or aircraft factories, or follow mothers and elder sisters into the cotton mills, which will switch to the production of tarpaulins, parachutes and military uniforms.

When peace comes, they will still have their lives ahead of them. The eldest of them – born before all women had the vote – will come of age in time to cast her own vote in the political earthquake that will be the election of 1945. Most will marry and have children, and will find their experience of family life fundamentally shaped by the new National Health Service, by near full employment and by the proliferation of consumer goods. But they will also live lives that continue to be marked by economic deprivation, and they will have to work hard to hold their families together and to make ends meet.

And they will forget about the school essays that they wrote in 1937, which will be stored in the archive of the research organisation Mass Observation, waiting.

As historians of twentieth-century Britain, we had long been fascinated by the activities of Mass Observation, the organisation established in early 1937 by a group of left-leaning intellectuals who wanted to create an 'anthropology of ourselves'. Over the next few years it sought out the views of thousands of ordinary people on everything from the prosaic to the profound, asking them to describe their experiences of a world that was changing around them.

We had immersed ourselves in its vast collection of material many times. We had read the stories of housewives, who told us about cobbling meals together on wartime rations alongside secret admissions of affairs. We had read young workers' descriptions of their dreams of the night before, or their opinions of radio shows and cinema releases; and the thoughts of retired men and women who reflected on the war, politics and the future, but also described the ornaments on their mantelpiece and the reasons for their choice of wallpaper.

But despite the variety of voices and eclecticism of the topics, the vast majority of material generated by the organisation was written by adults. Scholars from across the world have used the Mass Observation Archive to tell the history of modern Britain, but children are largely absent from their stories.

One day, in the summer of 2014 and while looking for something else, we stumbled across an entry in the online catalogue entitled 'Children's essays: observations in schools'. More recently, this collection has been digitised and can be quickly scanned at the click of a button. In 2014 it hadn't, but the archive is held at the Keep, near Brighton, a ten-minute walk from our University of Sussex campus. It was a sunny day and we were intrigued. We went to investigate.

We had no inkling of the volume of material we would find. Certainly, we were not prepared for the richness of the world that was revealed to us. It's rare to find historical sources written by children — especially working-class children. Historians seeking to reconstruct the experience of past childhoods usually have to rely on institutional records from orphanages, workhouses, religious, educational or charitable organisations and the like — in other words, sources written by adults. Alternatively, they use memoir and autobiographical sources; but these are written by the adults that children become, rather than the children they once were. Historical accounts written by children *while they were children* are scattered, scarce and fragmentary.

Yet here, in front of us, were thousands and thousands of pages, written by working-class girls and boys of all ages, giving us intimate snapshots of children's lives: their comments about their parents and friends, their hopes and fantasies, their daily routines.

We knew immediately the preciousness of what we were

looking at. The children's vivid descriptions told us about the tiniest details of their everyday lives but could also be used to illuminate the wider contradictions and challenges of life in 1930s Britain. This was what it felt like to grow up before the war.

Most of the essays were written by children living in Bolton or its surrounding towns, an area that Mass Observation studied in detail between 1937 and 1940. Using the pseudonym 'Worktown' in its reports, this was Mass Observation's first attempt to understand the everyday life of ordinary Britons. Several teachers were interested in getting involved and the collection of schoolchildren's essays was due to their willingness to extend Mass Observation's research into the classroom.

Almost all the children put their name on their work, and – as we read – we started to recognise repetitions. One particular class of twelve- and thirteen-year-old girls, Senior II at Pikes Lane Elementary School, was more prolific than others. On one occasion a teacher instructed them to 'Write the title "Heaven" and then tell me what you think about it. Don't ask me anything. Please put in your own thoughts and ideas.' This attempt to elicit sincere, or at least heartfelt, accounts echoed the advice that Mass Observation constantly offered when asking people to contribute to the organisation. Over the spring and summer of 1937, the Pikes Lane pupils composed several essays with titles such as 'How I spent my holidays', 'The Royal Family' and 'What I learn at home that I don't learn at school'.

As we traced the thoughts of individual girls across different topics, we started to get to know them – and to care about them. They wrote passionately and articulately, telling us about what they did, what they thought about and how they felt. We read the essays of twelve-year-old Madge, who aspired to be an author when she grew up and spent her spare time 'trying to make up good sensible poems'. Her ideas were independent and forthright. Writing about 'Hell' she noted of the Devil that 'people say he burns you in a fire but I don't say that it's true . . . He, the man who has no power, is trying all he can to take God's.'

Her writing had an immediacy that cut across the eight decades that separated us. Describing an imagined future as a farm worker, she asked us to 'just think how nice the fresh cream would be. Anyone who reads this I hope it does not make your mouth water as it has made mine.'

It felt like she was speaking directly to us. And it was about to get better.

As part of its study of Bolton, Mass Observation employed investigators to study ordinary people. One of them was a young man named Frank Cawson, fresh from Oxford and interested in education. He was delegated to find out more about the school. As part of his research, he made a number of pen sketches of the Pikes Lane children, writing their names beside each description.

About one girl, he commented: 'Father lorry driver, swears a lot. Spoil v scold. Mother admits can't manage her. Very funny looking. Father made her stick up for herself. Very pugnacious. Plausible, telltale. Very unpopular, the crooner at the concert. Untidy clothes.'

He was describing Madge.

*

We were troubled by the contrast between Cawson's careless comments and Madge's articulate and neatly-written essays. There was surely more to her than his cold and rushed appraisal suggested – this was a girl who had told us that what she appreciated most in others was friendship, love and kindness.

We wanted to know more. Who were these children of whom we'd become so fond? Could we reconstruct what their lives were like? We became obsessed with trying to find out. We subscribed to genealogy sites and sought out as many details as we could – where had the girls been born? Did they have brothers and sisters? What did their parents do? We searched the 1939 register, an official survey of the English and Welsh civilian population conducted just after the outbreak of war for the purpose of allocating ration books, which told us what the girls were doing in the immediate months after they left school. We went to the local archives in Bolton, looked through the school's records, pored over old photographs of the town. We walked the streets where they'd lived, sat in the park where they'd played and peered through the gates of Pikes Lane School.

Finally, we sought out their descendants. We hired a genealogist to do some discovery work. Infected by the same enthusiasm as us, she replied virtually overnight with the first few names and addresses and eventually managed to track down possible contacts for a good number of the class.

The archivists at Mass Observation were excited too. They willingly sent off letters on our behalf. We crossed our fingers and held our breath.

The waiting didn't last long. Within a couple of weeks around a dozen relatives had got back to us, and we planned a three-day trip north so we could visit and chat. Madge's daughter lived in Southport, an hour's drive away from Bolton – and we couldn't miss out on the chance to meet Madge's daughter – but most still lived within spitting distance of the town. Meanwhile families continued to get in touch. Soon there were too many to see in one trip, and so we planned for a second.

But it was now early March 2020 and things were starting to look very different. Horrendous reports were coming in of steeply rising death rates and overwhelmed health care systems elsewhere in the world. By mid-March, about the time that the World Health Organisation declared the COVID-19 outbreak to be a global pandemic, we knew we had to postpone. We had been due to go to Bolton on 21 March – Mothers' Day weekend. On 23 March, Prime Minister Boris Johnson announced the first national lockdown.

In the end, we were able to talk to relatives anyway, mostly on the phone, although some were willing to give Skype or Zoom a go. At last we could find out a bit more about the Pikes Lane girls and connect their childhood dreams with their lives as lived. 'What do you remember about them?' we asked their families. 'Did they find happiness and were they satisfied with the way their lives turned out? And did they ever talk about their years at Pikes Lane?'

This book is about what we discovered.

The Girls

(according to Mass Observer Frank Cawson).
Main characters, in order of appearance:

Madge: three children, the middle. Father lorry driver, swears a lot. Spoil v scold. Mother admits can't manage her. Very funny looking. Father made her stick up for herself. Very pugnacious. Plausible, telltale. Very unpopular. The crooner at the concert. Untidy clothes.

Mavis: one sister, one brother, one grown up sister (tuberculosis). Father working away. Average home, quite neatly dressed. Don't often go to Church. Often giddy. V thoughtful. Good at dancing. Rather bad eyesight. Quite popular ('the doubter').

Jessie: one of two sisters. Sophisticated. Father a labourer. Mother works in mill. Good at sports. Interested in boys. Tap dancing lessons. Good swimmer. Great initiative. Good at dramatics. Must be on front page. Much freedom at home. Good appearance, well groomed.

Amelia: one of two sisters. Nice child. Father window cleaner, very religious. Reads bible and things like that. Very quiet. Neat appearance. Works hard.

Molly: Only child. Father at Brewery. Intelligent. Learns piano privately. Five times to cinema a week. Grandmother dotes. Nice child. Dresses well. Very proud of child. Affable mother. Went away for holiday.

Irene: One of two children. Mother just had baby. Very spoilt. Father a spinner. Money to spend. Good at sports. Corporation house. Mother quite young. Went away to Southport. Father nondescript. Likes Morris Dancing.

Joyce D: three other children. She the eldest. Father a carter, gets up very early. Very nice in class, rather poorly dressed. Very poor vocabulary.

Dora: Many in family. Youngest child. Very fat and unattractive. Likeable. Clumsy. Father dead, used to clean buses. Very untidily dressed. Hates drawing. Loud voice. Keen on playing tunes on piano with one finger. Good natured. Cinema fan.

Annie: Two sisters and an older brother. Average working class. Clean. Very precocious. Well behaved. Neat appearance. Attends Pocket Mission.

Joan: Two in family. Mother died. Nicely off. Grandmother does well for them. Rather shy, not at all pushing. Reads a lot. Good looks. Refined. Father works in mill. Well kept. Mother used to work. Very proud of her. Good all round, good.

Marion: One sister, mother expecting another. Father injured in war, gets pension. Very good at sports. Nicely behaved. Once had nervous trouble. Salvation Army.

Mary: Very big family. Have allotment, live in the Pocket, not at all well off. Goes to the Clinic for everything. Most of kids work in mill. Reads a lot.

Elsie: eight children in family aged four to nineteen. One boy, rest girls, some at mill. Father unemployed. Good literary style. Mother anaemic, swears a lot. All family are together in very small house. Clever, very good looking, makes most of clothes, witty, popular. Excellent at debates.

Nellie: one brother. Father works on railway. Quite nice home. Pet rabbits and spaniel. Parents kind to her. Good appearance and well behaved. Good at sums.

Alice: Best friends with Elsie. Illegitimate. Very refined. Lives in flat with mother, who works in mill. Very good at art. Aunts take great interest. Good at nature study. Likes using big words, not a good speller. Good dancer, won first prize. Mixes with lots of boys, friends of cousin. Great pals with mother. Go about together. Go away for weekends together. Says Miss Kemp 'understands her'.

Joyce H: One brother. Poor health. Very pally with grandma. Nerve trouble. Very quiet. Nicely dressed. Average spending money.

Constance: Only child. Father works in mill. Mother too. Well dressed. Good condition. Plump. Parents very kind to her. Looks after auntie's baby. Went away and learnt to swim.

The Mass Observers

what the girls might have thought

Those who worked for Mass Observation would have seemed very distant to the girls. Its founders, Tom Harrisson and Charles Madge, both came from privileged backgrounds. Harrisson had been educated at Harrow, Madge at Winchester, both worlds away from Pikes Lane. Other Observers had also been privately and/or Oxbridge educated – men such as Brian Barefoot, Frank Cawson, John Sommerfield, Humphrey Spender and a handful of women such as Zita Baker and Penelope Barlow. Cawson and Barlow were at least Lancashire-born.

But there were also Mass Observers whose backgrounds were more similar to that of the girls. Walter Hood had grown up in a Durham mining community and came to Mass Observation via Labour politics and Ruskin College; Joe Wilcock and Tom Binks both came from working-class Lancashire families. And there were a host of local men and women who were involved more peripherally – people like Miss Kemp, Miss Taylor and Bill Naughton.

There is no suggestion that the Pikes Lane girls knew much – if anything – about Mass Observation's activities. Where they noticed the investigators taking notes, making lists, and recording overheard conversations verbatim, they may have thought it odd. If they saw Humphrey Spender, Mass Observation's photographer, taking shots of street scenes, millworkers or children's games, they might have considered the subjects to be rather mundane (though we have Spender to thank for most of the images of Bolton and Blackpool reproduced in this book). Had they ever read the rest of the accumulated research that Mass Observation produced, they would surely have been interested in the details of their home town. They might also have found at least some of it rather patronising.

1

Pikes Lane

A Mass Observer stands on a street corner, notebook, pen and camera in hand, outside the entrance to Pikes Lane Elementary School. He'd been there earlier that day to see the pupils arrive and had attracted their curiosity; children had clustered around him, wanting to know what he was doing. Now it is noon and he is waiting for them to come out for their dinner break. He has chosen a more discreet spot this time.

The girls are let out first, then one or two boys appear, and soon children are tumbling out of the school gates. Most of them have coats, he notices, although it is a warm day in early June, and he counts only ten children who wear them 'properly'; most have them unbuttoned or let them hang loosely on their shoulders. None seem in a particular hurry to get home and they jostle and call across to each other.

Several of the girls are carrying skipping ropes and the boys throw paper aeroplanes. One boy has a catapult, and later the Observer files away a newspaper report which blames the eight hundred plus broken panes of glass in Bolton's streetlamps – and a bill of over one hundred pounds to the council – on the catapult craze among the town's young male population.

There are a few mothers holding little ones or pushing prams, but a policeman is also there to see the children safely across the road. The Observer's eye is caught by a neatly dressed girl in a blue coat, with glasses and bobbed black hair. He watches her and a friend dawdle away from the school, one throwing her arms across the other's shoulders.

Another girl yells after them and chases to catch up. This one has 'a peculiar idea of walking with her coat over her head for a second or two – just lifting it up like a bird twice or thrice then walking a few yards and doing it again', he writes. They stop on the corner and chat for a moment before one peels away. The remaining two continue down the road, one skipping on and off the pavement as she goes.

They pause to coo over a baby, and then the friend enters a house. The girl in blue is the last remaining. She lives just one street further on, and the Observer watches her disappear into number 7, where her dinner will be waiting for her.

The girl is twelve-year-old Mavis, one of forty-one girls who make up the class of Senior II at the school. When another Mass Observer, Frank Cawson, later makes his pen sketches of the Pikes Lane girls, he will be complimentary about Mavis, describing her as very thoughtful, good at dancing and popular, even if she is 'often giddy'.

The Observer stays on duty to watch the children arrive back after their midday dinner. They'd hardly hurried home, he thinks, but they seem in even less of a rush to get back to lessons. As children dribble back in twos and threes, a group of girls start a game of rounders in the playground. Others play leapfrog or hopscotch. The boys prefer to chase one another, jumping on each other's backs and falling to the ground in a tangle. Some of the smaller children have sweets. One is sharing his toffees with others.

The blast of a whistle freezes the action. A couple of girls – hidden from the teacher by the L-shaped playground – continue to throw a ball until a second whistle prompts them to stop. 'All ran helter-skelter to a covered-in porch, lined up and marched off into school.'

Pikes Lane Elementary School opened in 1875. It was one of a new generation of school buildings built in the wake of the 1870 Education Act, after which the state systematically began to fund education for working-class children, a task previously left to charitable bodies or churches. As new schools appeared across the country, their distinctive architecture – bell towers, large windows and gabled ends – stood as symbols of Victorian efficiency and patrician intent; 'sermons in brick', as one London architect described them.

In the 1890s, Sir Arthur Conan Doyle wrote of Sherlock Holmes looking down over London from a train viaduct. The schools peppered the landscape, 'rising up above the slates, like brick islands in a lead-coloured sea'.

'Lighthouses my boy!' Holmes exclaimed to Watson. 'Beacons of the future! Capsules with hundreds of little bright seeds in each, out of which will spring the wise, better England of the future.'

In Bolton, the buildings vied for the skyline with the

mills – those other bricked symbols of nineteenth-century industriousness.

By 1937, there were more than seven hundred children at Pikes Lane: over two hundred seniors, divided into three classes of girls and three of boys; two hundred juniors; and three hundred infants, the latter accommodated in a separate building across the road. The school buildings had started to fray around the edges; a council survey of school premises described it as an 'old rambling building', in need of renovations.

But as the children disappeared through the heavy school doors and scattered to their different classrooms, they were performing a choreography unchanged, in its essence, for over sixty years. The school corridors were worn with the tread of generations of children and Mavis probably walked the same passages that her parents had done at the turn of the century. Her grandparents had come to Bolton as young teenagers with their families in the 1860s and '70s. They were by then too old to attend the school that they would have seen being built, though their younger siblings – Mavis's great uncles and aunts – would have done.

The fabric of the school was layered with the memories of children past, from the illicit graffiti on desks to the stains and marks made by inky fingers or scuffed feet. Pikes Lane likely had an honours board in its hall – many schools did in the 1930s – on which the names of notable past scholars were inscribed. It may also have had a roll of honour to commemorate the 'old boy heroes' who had served and died in the war. If so, Mavis would have seen the name of her uncle, the baby of her father's large family, who had died at Pozières in 1918, three weeks after his nineteenth birthday. There were other ways to remember a person, too – her older brother, born in 1920, had been given his uncle's name in his memory.

Earlier that morning, the school day had begun as normal with children clattering through the corridors and the walls rattling with the shouts and the noise. Pleas for children to come to school in lighter shoes have not had much success, particularly among the boys, and many are wearing clogs or heavy nailed boots.

Senior II's teacher is standing at the top of the stairs, watching her girls arrive. Some are energised and happy and they come bounding up the steps. Others are slower, less excited at the prospect of lessons. Three or four of the girls cluster around the passage windows that overlook the boys' yard. If no member of staff is about they will stand and wave, but today they snatch only a quick glance; they see their teacher watching and move on, giving her wry grins as they pass.

One of the girls is thirteen-year-old Jessie. She is 'rather keen on boys, has simply masses of self-confidence and loves to show off', according to her teacher. Later that afternoon, Jessie and a couple of others will get into trouble when they are caught throwing a ball from their playground up to the boys' classroom window. The girls will only get 'ticked off', though – the boys egging them on will be caned.

In the classroom, there is a hubbub of noisy chatter. Mirrors are taken out and hair is combed. Several tell their teacher about the man outside: 'We have had our photos taken.' They seem pleased and are taking more care over their appearance than normal, she thinks, perhaps anticipating further photographs later in the day. One girl comes to the front to confess to forgetting her spellings. They have twenty to learn each week and any done incorrectly have to be written out fifty times. She *must* bring them in for the afternoon session, her teacher warns her. All sit for the milk register – several children in the class qualify for free milk, and others pay – and then into the hall for prayers. There seems to be little concentration; one or two don't even bother to close their eyes.

After assembly, the first lesson of the day is scripture and the children are making notes on the destruction of Jerusalem. There is some amusement over the names of the kings – 'what sort of name is Nebuchadnezzar?!' – but that diversion only lasts so long. 'Have we to do *all* this?' asks one, raising her eyebrows at the length of the chapter. She heaves a sigh and gets back to work.

Soon they are restless. There is only one Bible between two, which doesn't help concentration. 'Some pull and push the books about and are generally rather peevish,' the teacher writes. One girl gets bored and takes her mirror out again to examine her lips and gums – 'but they're bleeding!' At the end of the lesson there are arguments over which girl should store the Bible. A pair at the back insist that both their desks are full. 'I said that one *had* to find room, so, at length, after much cramming down of book, room was found.'

Next is arithmetic, and the class are set to work on the long division of money fractions and decimals. 'What are my profits if I buy an article for eleven shillings and sixpence and sell it for thirteen shillings?' And then it's playtime. The teacher bows to pressure – 'please, miss' – and agrees to referee for them.

Jessie is as good at rounders as she is at every kind of sport, but she doesn't get much chance to shine today. Another girl's wild hit sends the ball flying onto the shed roof, and by the time a replacement is found the whistle has been blown.

Senior II's teacher was Dorothy Kemp. In 1937, she wasn't much older than her pupils. Miss Kemp, as they called her, had been born in 1913 and grown up at a house in Sterratt Street, a five-minute walk from Pikes Lane, which she almost certainly would have attended herself. Her family background was not unlike those of the children she taught: her father worked in the mill and her mother had been a dressmaker before marriage. But the young Dorothy wanted a different life. As a clever working-class girl growing up in interwar Britain her options were limited, but a career in teaching offered one way of avoiding the textile industry. After leaving school she enrolled at Edge Hill teaching college in nearby Ormskirk. In May 1934, not yet twenty-one, she joined Pikes Lane as a teacher.

The 1930s was an exciting time to be a young teacher. New, progressive ideas were spreading through the training colleges, where lecturers taught the value of hands-on activities and group work and spoke of the importance of relating academic endeavours to children's real lives and experiences.

Between 1923–33, a series of government-commissioned reports chaired by the educationalist Sir Henry Hadow advocated child-centred educational reform, suggesting that a good school 'is not a place of compulsory instruction but a community of old and young, engaged in learning by co-operative experiment'. In what became one of the most famous lines of the reports, it was stated that 'the curriculum is to be thought of in terms of activity and experience rather than knowledge to be acquired and facts to be stored'.

Miss Kemp would have lapped it up. She already thought of herself as proudly progressive – it was one of the reasons she wanted to get involved with Mass Observation, with its aim of studying the ordinary man or woman in the street, rather than royals, aristocrats or politicians.

Once they left college and entered the classroom, idealistic young teachers often found that theory was hard to put into practice: the restrictive physical layout of buildings, large class sizes and the sometimes suspicious attitudes of older colleagues or headteachers meant that it was often easier to fall back on more traditional methods. Rote learning and drilled testing, for example, remained important in Pikes Lane as in other schools, not least because of a system by which children moved up from class to class according to their ability to pass certain standards rather than their chronological age.

But that didn't mean that Miss Kemp had to like it. The day she recorded a diary for Mass Observation, Thursday 10 June, was in the middle of a week of testing. Her girls had a geography exam in the morning and a needlework exam in the afternoon. She added a caveat to the top of her account: 'I found it a very boring day as I was unable to take an oral lesson, so kids had much fewer opportunities to talk.'

The children are quieter on their return after morning play, a combination of disappointment over the aborted rounders game and anticipation of the geography exam to come. All belongings are put away and only pens, blotting paper and ink are allowed on the desk. Miss Kemp asks the children to prop the big books – the ones they usually use for painting – upright between them so they can't see each other's papers. 'Oh, Miss Kemp, we weren't going to copy,' protests Jessie innocently – she is a good actor as well – when she is pulled up for sneaking a seat next to her best friend, Amelia. 'I'm very glad to hear it,' replies Miss Kemp, but moves her back to her usual place all the same.

Each child is given a hectographed map of Africa. They are asked to label the five rivers that have been drawn on – the Nile, Niger, Zambezi, Congo and Orange Rivers – and then name some of the marked countries and principal towns of what was then known as British Africa. Ten short questions follow ('Give two products of the Sudan'; 'What town does Table Mountain overlook?'). The main question, for a full ten marks, asks for an account of one of the following: Nigeria, Zanzibar or Malaya. Most of the children choose to write about the latter as the country most fresh in their mind, the class having gathered around the school's wireless set earlier that week to listen to the BBC's educational broadcast on the country.

Miss Kemp describes the scene: 'Some chewed pen ends – yawns – staring into distance – fixed expressions – wrinkling up nose – screwing up eyes – scratching chin – occasional heavy sighs.' One girl whispers to another and 'I jumped on her at once: "What did you say?" "It's alright, miss," says the other. "She only said she hadn't finished yet."'

Whenever a girl turns a page there is a ripple of movement across the room as all turn, interested in how much others are writing. Within an hour they're starting to tire. Those who finish are allowed to hand their papers in and choose a library book from the shelf to read quietly. Most find this a preferable activity and are trying to finish off as quickly as possible.

'Miss Kemp, was it at Mombasa the natives used dhows?' asks Jessie, referring to the Arab sailing vessels they'd talked about in class.

'I'm very sorry but this is a test and of course I can't answer a question like that.'

Jessie grins and bends her head over her work again.

2.

Expectations

Molly doesn't mind the test. She is quiet and studious and works hard at school. She likes being in the classroom and is fond of her teacher too. When she is asked what she would like to do when she grows up, she replies, 'I would choose to be a teacher at Pikes Lane. I should like to teach Senior II and be a nice teacher like Miss Kemp.'

It's Molly's thirteenth birthday in a couple of weeks. Her parents will spoil her, as they are wont to do. Asked in class what her favourite foods are, she lists chicken or steak puddings and fancy cakes. Maybe she'll be treated to these for her birthday tea.

She belongs to a close and loving little family, sharing a terraced house with her parents and widowed grandmother ('grandmother dotes', writes Cawson in his pen sketch). But Molly hates being an only child, even if their home is rarely quiet. Her mum loves company and there are always friends and family round. Molly is the same. She'll always want people around her.

If she misses having brothers or sisters, at least one of the benefits is that money is not as tight as it is for other classmates. Both her parents work, and they can even afford to send her for private piano lessons. She loves to play, though she won't continue with it beyond childhood. Later in life she'll often wish for a bigger house, with space for a piano.

In the absence of younger siblings, smaller children are easy to find in the park or street and are usually happy enough to be co-opted into playing the pupils' roles in a game of schools. 'I should like to be a teacher because I like teaching and marking books,' writes Molly. 'There are so many things to learn. I would choose arithmetic, composition and English for those are the subjects I like.'

She imagines being in charge of a classroom and suggests that 'all round the walls I would hang pictures of famous writers and have a noticeboard with the world affairs on', presumably modelling the look on her own experience at Pikes Lane.

She would no doubt have kept a tight ship. Deference towards authority is something she will insist on for the rest of her life: 'you sit well, you behave, you don't question the teacher, doctor or policeman' is something she will drill into her own children. She can claim that it's in her blood. Her great-grandfather had been the chief constable of Bolton in the 1870s, living at 79a Davenport Street until his death in the 1890s. The house was just a couple of doors down from number 85, where, forty-odd years later, Mass Observation will set up its headquarters.

Molly wasn't the only girl in the class who wanted to be a teacher when she grew up. Irene told Miss Kemp that her first choice would be to become 'a queen', but, failing that, she thought teaching would be a good job. Not only would she get a decent wage, but the career prospects were attractive too. 'I should like to be a teacher because when you have been there a long time you have a good chance to be headmistress of the school,' she explained.

As she wrote her fantasy, she started to live it, imagining it so hard that her writing slipped into the past tense: 'When I went to be a teacher I had to have training. I learned training at college.'

Irene's home situation was similar to Molly's. She was also an only child – at least for the moment; her mother was expecting again. Like Molly, both her parents worked, her father at the foundry, her mother at the mill. She's spoilt, Cawson said of Irene when he made his pen sketch, adding in an aside that, from him, didn't sound like a compliment: 'money to spend'.

Perhaps it was their relatively more prosperous circumstances that meant these two girls dared to dream about a career into which they had little chance of entry. Like most British children of the period, Molly and Irene had been at Pikes Lane Elementary School since their infant years and would stay there until the age of fourteen. They had graduated to the senior classes for their final years but would never leave the elementary school.

Attendance at a dedicated secondary school was for those who could afford to pay or for those working-class children who were able to win a free place at the age of eleven. Bolton LEA was generous in its supply of free place scholarships, and a relatively high proportion of Pikes Lane juniors were successful in moving on. Those who didn't, and were left in the senior classes – Molly, Irene and their classmates – were described by one school inspector as 'the residue'.

A teaching certificate required a secondary education followed by further college training – as Irene had explained. She knew the kind of education that went on at a secondary school. 'If I were a teacher at the high school, I would teach boys and girls shorthand and a foreign language,' she wrote, despite the fact that these were both subjects unavailable to her at Pikes Lane. Like other elementary schools, it lacked the facilities of its secondary counterparts. A 1934 inspection report of Pikes Lane School had criticised the absence of dedicated classrooms for girls to do science or special craft work.

But not all children who won scholarships took up their secondary school places. A secondary education entailed expenses other than fees, and the purchase of books and uniform might be beyond the means of some families. Even more of a sacrifice was the delay in a child starting to bring in earnings. Elementary school children finished their education at fourteen; secondary schools taught pupils up to the age of sixteen and beyond. It meant at least an extra two years in which a son or daughter would not be contributing to the household budget. With the best will in the world, the financial pressures might be insurmountable.

Joyce D – one of four Joyces in the class – enjoys school like Molly and Irene, although she has the same dislike of homework as any twelve-year-old. 'It stops you from going out to play or going to the pictures,' she writes in one of her school essays.

But for Joyce there is an added pressure, for her

parents aren't keen on her spending too much time on her schoolwork either. 'My teacher says we should do homework "because we learn better",' Joyce reports, 'but my mother tells me not to do it; she says that we have enough to do in school.' Joyce is torn between her two grown-ups and their contradictory demands. She eventually finds a way to keep them both happy: 'I go upstairs and do it when my mother does not know where I am.'

Joyce's mother's resentment of the time spent on schoolwork is probably at least partly due to her reliance on her eldest daughter for help with the housework, which never seems to end. There are three younger children in the family, including a new baby, and everyone is expected to chip in as soon as they're old enough. 'I go on errands every day,' writes Joyce in another school essay, explaining proudly that 'when you begin to go errands your father or mother writes it on a piece of paper but as you grow older you will know what you want.'

She lists a number of jobs that she might also do during the week – mopping the kitchen, minding the baby, polishing the dresser, washing up or 'putting the pots in a neat order to make them look pretty'. She likes cooking the best, making 'fruit pies for Sunday's tea' or baking bread or cakes.

But her mother's attitude is also rooted in her expectation of Joyce's future – for what is the point of spending time on schoolwork when there will be so little use for it? Homework is unusual for elementary schoolchildren, but Joyce had been in the top class the previous year, working towards the scholarship examination. In this class the teachers had encouraged home learning, sending spellings and poetry home for children to practise.

We don't know whether Joyce did well enough in the examination to win a free place or not, but if she did then it seems her parents turned it down; at any rate, she is still at Pikes Lane in 1937. But committing to two more years of schooling would have been impossible. Her father is unemployed, and money is tight. For her family, who need her earnings, her fourteenth birthday can't come soon enough. She will start work as a bristle sorter at the mill when she leaves school at the end of 1938.

Joyce wasn't the only girl to feel conflicted between the expectations placed on her by her teacher and the different priorities of her family. In August, Miss Kemp set her class an essay entitled 'What I learn at home that I don't learn at school', and it's clear from the girls' answers that there wasn't always an easy relationship between the two.

Dora, another classmate, often found herself caught up in a similar dilemma, something she was smart enough to capture in just a couple of sentences. 'Sometimes the teacher says, "take your books out", but at home, my mother will say, "Put your book away and go me an errand",' she explained. 'If you are speaking when there is a lesson on, the teacher gives you a hundred lines, but my mother says, "You will have to wash up those cups and saucers and put them away, you little monkey."'

Even if mothers accepted the authority of school staff in the training of their daughters in reading, writing and arithmetic, they might have other objections. 'When I told my mother we have to take our own pens, she said, "we pay taxes for things like these",' Madge told Miss Kemp.

Mothers were certainly less likely to accept that the

teachers knew best when it came to domestic subjects. 'At school we are learned how to wash clothes but our mothers teach us how they were taught so we do not learn as much at school as we do at home,' wrote another child. Madge had taken some cakes home once, and her mother had been fiercely critical. She should have used a quarter of a teaspoon of bicarbonate of soda, not a half – and why had she not used egg? Why a full teaspoon of cream of tartar? Irene's mother had been similarly unimpressed: 'My mother shows me another way how to make the cakes I have learned at school.'

Mothers might also take exception to the assumption that a school's job was to teach its pupils good character and manners, with the implication that mothers weren't doing a good enough job in this themselves.

Across many deprived areas of Britain in the 1930s, schools were represented by middle-class educationalists, politicians and journalists as a 'civilising' force in working-class communities, trying to do good work in difficult circumstances. An inspector's comment on Pikes Lane boys' department a few years previously – that 'the social conditions of the locality are none too encouraging or helpful' – was typically dismissive. The report of the girls' department attributed the good conduct of the children to the influence of the school: 'The admirable manners which the girls have acquired reflect great credit on all concerned.'

And yet the girls' essays showed that there were limits to what the school could teach: that 'teachers cannot show us how to use a knife and fork and our manners at the table', for example. Nor were manners or character an area that their mothers neglected. 'At home I am taught my manners and not to use vulgar words,' wrote one girl, the daughter of an unemployed mill labourer. 'I have to be ladylike and polite, when I am asked a question I have to look at the person who asks the question and answer properly.' Such training was exactly what middle-class inspectors praised, but few of them expected it to be insisted upon within such a family.

Some of the conflict came over what counted as good manners and particularly – another obsession of the inspectors – good speech. The way children were encouraged to speak at school was often different to the way they spoke in the street, to the extent that some school inspectors referred to working-class children as 'bilingual'.

For if children learnt to soften their accents and watch their dialect while they were in the classroom, it was seen as putting on airs and graces if they did the same at home. 'The teacher learns us speech training and my mother contradicts me,' wrote Irene. Madge's mother was particularly concerned about what others might think. 'My mother is always shouting and saying, "don't talk swanky when we have relatives here, never mind what they learn you at school. You are up at school to work, learning to spell, read, write and do sums, not to waste your time learning swanky talk."'

Before the Mass Observer left his spot outside the gates of Pikes Lane, he had watched a class of girls receive a lesson in deportment, which took place in the yard. Five at a time, the girls walked with a book on their heads, stepping over and then under a length of string. 'They all seemed to enjoy this,' he commented. One imagines that their mothers would have thought it a complete waste of time.

*

Had Joyce been born just a few years later, things would have been different. The British school system was shortly to change. The 1944 Education Act would finally abolish fees for secondary schools and raise the school leaving age to fifteen, opening up four years of dedicated secondary education to all children, regardless of their ability to pay.

Even before this, local education authorities had been rethinking the way that schools were organised, with a push from the late 1920s onwards for a clearer division within the elementary system between junior education before the age of eleven, and senior education after it. Bolton's elementary schools were 'solidly built', the town's educationalists in the 1930s reflected; 'admirable in their own way but quite unsuitable for modern requirements'.

And so Bolton began a three-year scheme of reorganisation in 1936, designating the council's elementary schools either junior or senior, and transferring pupils accordingly. In September 1937, the older girls of Pikes Lane were moved to Derby Street School for Senior Girls; its older boys to White Bank School, now for Senior Boys. Pikes Lane, now to be a junior school, took the younger children from Derby Street and White Bank in return.

Molly is only at Derby Street for a year. When she leaves in July 1938, aged fourteen, she takes home a school leaving report. She has made marked improvement in every way, records her teacher, 'doing some excellent work in Geography while her practical subjects were always neatly and carefully done'. She had found a natural position as a school monitor, in which she had always been 'very willing and helpful'.

'Our best wishes go with her on starting work,' finishes the report. And start work she does, at a local book-binding firm. Her fleeting fantasy of becoming a teacher fades – though later, as a mother of six children, it'll sometimes feel like she's halfway to doing the job anyway. She continues to love books for the rest of her life – Agatha Christie will be her favourite author – and will bring up all her children to be readers.

Her three eldest, all boys, will themselves go to Pikes Lane. When we speak to her daughter, child number four, she tells us one of her earliest memories. She is standing beside her mother at the school gate at breaktime with a drink and piece of toast for one of the boys. He won't drink the school milk and Molly can't bear the thought of him going hungry.

Irene, like Joyce, starts work at the mill when she leaves school. She, too, will continue to value education. 'She taught me a hell of a lot,' Irene's son will tell us, as he remembers her putting him through his paces in reading and writing after getting back from a long day at work. Just as her mother was with her, Irene will be a teacher in the kitchen too, and he 'will know his way around a cooking board' when he's still very small.

As for Joyce's children, they don't have to hide their learning from their mother. She will insist on them doing their homework and doing it well. She doesn't want them to end up in a factory like her, and they won't.

3.

The Pictures

Molly wakes on the morning of Good Friday to the other-worldly stillness of an overnight snowfall. She frowns – this wasn't the plan. But she's not going to stay in. 'I was amazed to find it had been snowing but it did not stop me from going for a walk,' she writes later. Even in her old age, her daughter will tell us, Molly was a woman who hated being stuck in the house.

Molly and Flora are off to the Jumbles today, the beautiful area of countryside to the north of Bolton, and the two friends are determined to enjoy themselves, whatever the weather. 'We walked by a river till we got to the only cottages we could see. We had our tea then played games and admired the trees, birds and many other things,' writes Flora, and Molly is pleased when they find 'a nice cosy spot near a river' to sit.

By late afternoon they are heading home to a drink and some hot cross buns, cold-fingered and -toed but red-cheeked and smiling. 'Everybody should have hot cross buns on Good Friday,' says Molly, another ritual that she will carry with her for the rest of her life.

After the day spent outdoors, the dark warmth of the cinema appeals. That evening, the two girls are off to the Rialto, which advertises itself as 'the cinema where you meet your friends'. They see the 1936 crime drama *Charlie Chan at the Racetrack*, and it's eleven o'clock before they get home.

The next day, Saturday, sees the two of them together again at the Queen's cinema, built before the First World War. It is another regular haunt of many of the girls and – according to local boy and future film critic Leslie Halliwell – it smells of 'soft plush and worn carpets and Devon violets and sweat'. The picture is the comedy *The Man Who Could Work Miracles*, based on H. G. Wells's fantasy novel.

Sunday 'is the best day' though, declares Molly, because of the Easter eggs. She gets five and listens to the Easter service on the wireless. No cinemas are open on a Sunday, but on Easter Monday she's back with Flora and this time it's to the Regal to see a western, *The Texas Rangers*. The Regal is on the other side of the railway tracks to Pikes Lane and a short walk from Molly's house. For the moment it is Bolton's largest cinema (the Odeon, which will open later in the year, will be bigger), and the back stalls are 'so far away from the screen that you needed a telescope to find out what was going on'.

Molly's fourth and final cinema of the long Easter weekend is the Embassy, across the way from Woolworths in the town centre. It was the one of the first cinemas to open in Bolton in 1910, and it's now showing its age. She and Flora have spent that morning trying to trick each other with April Fools (Flora caught me, Molly concedes; I caught everyone, Flora boasts); they go to see the romantic musical comedy *Happiness Ahead* in the afternoon, and finish off the holiday that evening with a game of rounders in the park.

When the Mass Observers arrived in Bolton in 1937, a study of the cinema was high on their list of priorities. 'No study of life in an industrial town, for that matter in any community in Western civilisation, would be complete without it', they explained.

It was, after all, a decade in which new forms of commercialised leisure – with the cinema foremost among them – were changing the feel of British society. When the novelist and playwright J. B. Priestley wrote a travelogue of his journey around England a few years previously, he had described signs of a 'new' England in the making. Different to the rural England of little villages nestled among country lanes, and different again to the industrial England of tightly packed workers' housing overlooked by factory chimneys or pit shafts, this was an England of consumption and leisure, with dance halls, chain stores, cafés and cinemas, of 'factory girls looking like actresses . . . and everything given away for cigarette coupons'.

In a decade of significant political and economic division, the cinema had near-universal appeal. There were 946 million cinema tickets sold in the UK in 1937 (compared to 176 million in 2019). Residents of Bolton could choose between twenty-two cinemas in the 1930s; there were nearly fifty within a radius of five miles. It was, recalled Leslie Halliwell later, 'almost like mecca' for filmgoers.

When the manager of the Embassy – a 'fair-haired, drunken-looking man of middle age' – spoke to Mass Observation, he told them that Bolton's working people 'don't think they've been anywhere if they haven't been to the cinema twice a week'. He went on to echo Priestley: 'They're working all day, and they come up here at night all dressed up like dandies. They think they're on top of the Earth, you've got to make them think that they are.'

The Observers also tried to speak to the manager of the Queen's, but he was suspicious of their attempts to elicit information. They dismissed him summarily in turn: 'Cold, discourteous, disagreeable. Unresponsive to usual social artifices. A bastard. Won't even give us a list of films.'

6 May 1937 is Ascension Day, and the extra day off school is used by many of the girls to go to the pictures just as they'd done over the Easter weekend. Annie, just turned thirteen, initially forgets that Pikes Lane is closed. 'I jumped out of bed at half past seven, then I got myself ready,' she writes. 'At half past eight I went across to a shop for some biscuits for my lunch, I had quite forgot we had a holiday. When I got to the top of our street, I thought everything was quiet, then I remembered.'

She doubles back to tell her mother before heading off for rounders and hopscotch in the park, taking along her neighbour's baby whom she's been asked to mind. After lunch she goes to the Windsor cinema, minutes from the school and a stone's throw from her house on Balshaw Street. It had once been a Methodist chapel but was converted to a picture house in the late 1920s.

It was a 'small and spiritless' place, according to Halliwell, notwithstanding its holy ancestry and despite its redecoration and renaming as the Windsor that year, in honour of the coronation. Annie takes the baby there too, hoping that the darkness and the warmth will encourage sleep. It doesn't, and the child's crying continues. Annie takes her home and returns to catch the end of the picture on her own.

While Annie is trying to hush the baby, Joan can be found in the centre of town, at the Capitol on Churchgate. For the time being at least, the Capitol claims to be the grandest cinema in Bolton, with a royal circle as well as a balcony and stalls, plus a café. Her child's ticket for the matinee performance sets Joan back fourpence (or she could have paid an extra tuppence for a circle seat). This is about half her weekly spending money, most of it given to her by her grandma or earnt in chores. She usually saves the rest to spend on sweets. If she has to queue that day, as you usually do at the Capitol, then Ye Olde Pastie Shoppe a few doors down, with its famous meat-and-potato turnovers, will tempt her too; potato pie is one of her favourites. But the waiting isn't too bad – as she gets nearer she can listen to the end of the last film through the cinema wall.

The details the girls give on how they spend their pocket money is a good indication of the importance they give to cinema attendance. Like Joan, Madge divides hers between sweets (usually toffees) and the pictures. She also has to budget a penny for the tram fare to get into town to visit the Lido, one of her favourite cinemas. The Lido had opened only that year, with the young Halliwell in attendance. He hadn't been able to see much of the screen but was appeased by sample packets of a new kind of sweet that the usherettes 'were practically throwing at everyone who came in'. They were called Maltesers, 'and I grabbed as many as I could from the tray on the way to my seat'.

For Molly, Annie, Joan, Madge and their friends, knowledge of film and of film stars is a given, not least because of the frequency with which they go to the cinema and the range of different films they see. When Miss Kemp asks the girls to name their favourite film, everyone is able to give an answer. The most popular is *Rose Marie*, a 1936 musical starring Nelson Eddy and Jeanette MacDonald. It is the story of an opera singer's romance with a Canadian Northwest Mountie, 'whose name she scarcely knew but whose caresses spoke the language of love'.

Both Annie and Joan give their favourite as the 1936 Oscar-nominated *Romeo and Juliet*, a MGM film starring 'First Lady of the Screen, the Lovely Norma Shearer', and Leslie Howard, 'the passionate dreamer and romantic lover'. *Variety* magazine called it a 'faithful' adaptation 'played sincerely and beautifully', but also found it 'not too imaginative' and implied that, at two hours, it was just a bit too long. Molly's favourite is the romantic comedy *Small Town Girl*; Madge prefers the tragic romance of *Dark Angel*.

Beyond these shared choices the girls had catholic tastes, mentioning anything from light British films such as *Sunshine Ahead*, through various genres such as 'cowboy pictures', to Hollywood classics such as *Showboat* and *Swingtime*. Musicals were particularly popular.

Nor were the girls stuck for an answer when asked to name their favourite cinema stars. Jean Harlow, Jeanette MacDonald and Robert Taylor were frequently mentioned, as were Clark Gable, Shirley Temple and Ginger Rogers.

Another girl in the class went to the cinema twice a week, and thought that when she grew up, she'd like to be a film actress 'like Ginger Rogers because you have lovely frocks and a lot of money and nice homes. I should like to live in New York where Fred Astaire is then we should go on the films together. We should have lovely frocks and we should be the principal of the film. We should be good dancers and we should dance together. We should have great fun with all the people watching us and saying what good dancers we are.'

Dora vies with Molly to be the most avid of Senior II's film fans. She is one of the oldest girls in the class, and Frank Cawson's description of her is one of his most brutal: 'Very fat and unattractive. Likeable. Clumsy. Father dead, used to clean buses. Very untidily dressed. Hates drawing. Loud voice. Keen on playing tunes on piano with one finger. Good natured.'

But Dora's inauspicious surroundings and the recent loss of her father have not dulled her fantasies, nor her ability to write about them. She is a particularly keen and knowledgeable film fan. Her favourite picture is *The Bride Walks Out*, a 1936 American comedy in which glamorous Carolyn (played by Barbara Stanwyck, Dora's favourite female star), struggles to accept restraints on her spending after having been forced by her husband to give up her job as a model. She tries working secretly, while also being courted by a wealthy playboy, though ultimately rejects both job and suitor and returns to her husband.

Dora might have preferred a different ending. Asked what she wants to be when she grows up, she replies, 'I want to be a millionaire and have a handsome young man for my husband.' She fantasises about travelling to America, where 'I would go to Hollywood and get a glimpse of the stars such as Norma Shearer, Robert Taylor, Shirley Temple and Jane Withers, who was in the film *Ginger*. I would stay there forever, if I had my choice.'

For Dora it is not to be. On leaving school she follows her older siblings into the mill as a cotton ring doffer, unloading the full bobbins from the machines. It's not quite the future she might have liked. Nor does she ever find her millionaire; in fact, she is one of the few Pikes Lanes girls who will never marry.

As part of its investigation into the cinema, Mass Observation conducted a more detailed survey in 1938. A questionnaire was handed to each patron buying a ticket at the Odeon, the Crompton or the Palladium; three cinemas in Bolton that catered to the top, middle and bottom of the market respectively. Two top prizes of one pound and complimentary tickets for six runners-up were promised for the 'best' answers, with the request that: 'We want to know what sort of Films you really like, and why? Remember, write down quite frankly what you feel are the most honest answers, do not bother about style or punctuation. This is not an English Essay competition . . .'

Mavis's Aunt Bessie is one of the 559 entrants. She knocks several years off her age and puts herself down as twenty-nine. Maybe she thinks that a twenty-something single woman has more chance of winning than a forty-something spinster (how – or indeed if – Mass Observation ever decided on the winners is not recorded). She lives with her younger brother on the other side of Bolton to Mavis, but she is close to her nephews and nieces – Mavis's younger sister is named after her.

Bessie is as avid a film fan as her niece, often attending three or four times a week. The appeal of the cinema cut across generational and gender divides in 1930s Britain, which was one reason for its success. For middle-aged women like Bessie, the opportunities for respectable leisure pursuits had previously been very limited.

Asked on her preference for British versus American films, Bessie declares that she likes both, although American ones could be 'a bit noisy'. Love stories and musical romances are her personal favourites – the latter is the most popular film type among all of those asked. When asked to pick from a list of what she'd like to see more of, she answers, 'One: more beautiful people. Two: more royalty and aristocrats. Three: more beautiful things.' (In this she differs, perhaps unsurprisingly, from a fourteen-year-old boy whose top request is for 'more killing'.)

Like others who filled out the questionnaire, Bessie's comments reflected the fact that a trip to the cinema was an experience that amounted to more than just the film. She singled out the Odeon's organist for particular praise: he 'simply thrills everyone'. His playing was a draw for several others, too, including children. As one twelve-year-old girl wrote, 'The Odeon cinema is the most comfortable picture-house in town. The organ is very beautiful, and when I get settled in one of the seats listening to the music, I feel that I could stay there for ever.'

The manager of the Embassy agreed that the experience mattered as much as the film and thought it one reason why small cinemas like his survived: 'I believe people don't like the big barns, they like to be in a crowd. You go in a great barn of a place. You go in when there's a bad picture, and a few people dotted about, and you feel lonely . . .'

Middle-class commentators of the period often worried about the influence of cinema and celebrity culture on the lives of working-class children. They feared that on-screen fantasies fuelled unrealistic hopes for the future and that the glamour of screen idols would make them feel dissatisfied with their own lives. In 1931, during a debate in Parliament about the Sunday opening of cinemas, a Conservative MP cited a survey from Birmingham, in which schoolchildren had been asked for their impressions upon leaving the cinema. They gave, he said, some shocking replies: 'How very easy it is to open safes', 'how the idle rich live', 'how very easy it is to deceive a policeman', 'what a very good time a girl can have'.

These fears weren't restricted to Members of Parliament, and many of Bolton's older generation worried that the cinema might have undesirable effects on the younger. One woman who answered Mass Observation's cinema questionnaire suggested that there should be fewer American pictures and more British ones to 'stop American twang among children'. Even Molly had a sense of cinema-going as an activity with a touch of the illicit about it. Asked what Heaven was like, she answered that it was 'just another world like the one we live on at present except that it might not have pictures and dance halls'.

None of the Pikes Lane girls answered the cinema survey, but the replies sent in by others show that young people were, in fact, able to separate out fiction from the everyday.

One teenage girl was sceptical of love movies: 'There is nothing real about them. People in real life would not do the silly things that film lovers do.' Another thought Westerns unrealistic: 'The hero keeps firing without reloading their gun, and in crime films the hero always escapes no matter what sort of a tight corner he is in.' Mavis's Aunt Bessie may have wanted to see 'more beautiful people', but a request for 'more people like you and I' was also common.

Others embraced the fantasy and recognised it for what it was. As one thirteen-year-old girl put it: 'People don't go to the pictures to see other people's troubles.'

The cinema remained important to the girls for years to come. Across the country, the popularity of the cinema continued to grow – ticket sales peaked at 1.64 billion a year in 1946. As a young mother, Annie never stopped loving her trips to the pictures. It became routine to take her little girl with her – as she'd once taken her neighbour's child – and regular family trips to see films together would later pattern her daughter's earliest childhood memories.

But by the time Annie's second child was born, seven years later, there was a new television in the corner of the living room and visits to the cinema dropped away. One by one the girls' haunts were first repurposed as bingo halls or skating rinks, before eventual demolition to make way for shops, offices or housing. The Regal, where Molly and Flora made one of their Easter weekend trips, was destroyed by fire in 1985 and is now the site of the Bolton Lads and Girls' Club.

But in 1937, the cinema was still modern, new and magical.

*

You can hear the music from several streets away, above the hubbub of the crowd. A handful of policemen are there, keeping a watchful eye, but the mood is affable. It is Saturday 21 August 1937, the opening night of the new 2,534-seater Odeon, the latest addition to Bolton's extensive range of picture houses, and the management are pulling out all the stops. The coloured tiles catch the neon lights and it seems as if the whole building is shimmering in the darkness, dancing along to the scarlet-clad bandsmen who are piping out their tunes.

A fifty-yard queue snakes down the street from the box office. For those lucky enough to secure a ticket the magic continues. They enter a picture palace, ushered in by attendants in evening dress and surrounded by gold paint, red velour curtains, fluted walls and a profusion of fresh flowers. Green octagonal clocks on the wall use capital letters – THE ODEON – instead of numerals, although in one misstep the Mass Observer who is there notices that one has stopped and will announce the time as 7.03 for the rest of the evening. The band have moved inside too and are now arrayed across the stage, rolling through their repertoire of dance favourites. Their percussionist wears a leopard skin.

The Mass Observer thinks that several filmgoers seem shy in the surroundings, and there is some nervous laughter. At least a couple of people end up on the floor, not expecting the seats to spring upwards as they sit, and there are pockets of amusement around the auditorium, as well as some muttering: 'They should tell folks, not make them look like fools.' As guests settle, bagpipes strike up and six kilted pipers fan down the aisles. Then everyone stands for the national anthem before the speeches begin.

First up is the cinema manager – 'I think you will find me very approachable. I come to Bolton as a crusader' – followed by various Odeon employees. Oscar Deutsch himself, founder of the Odeon chain, is away on 'some very urgent film business', but Harry Wheedon is there, the architect whose art deco designs will mark the Odeon brand for decades to come. Then Bolton's mayor – he's nervous, the Mass Observer thinks – declares the cinema open, hoping for 'good, clean and wholesome entertainment' and 'many pleasant evenings'. The speakers' wives are presented with bouquets by a stiff and self-conscious pageboy, whose rigid salute gets applause and laughter from the crowd.

The last introduction goes to Harry Croft, the organist 'who will be here to play to you every evening'. Croft plays for fifteen minutes, coloured lighting changing around him. He finishes to loud applause and, as the huge glass-sided Compton organ descends back into the orchestra pit, he throws up his left hand in acknowledgement and smiles round at the audience.

At last, the projector bursts into life. After a news short and a cartoon, the main feature is *Dark Journey*, featuring Conrad Veidt and newcomer Vivien Leigh. It 'is full of submarines, spies, discreet sex and flashy prostitutes', writes the Mass Observer later, noting also that there are several children sitting near him, including a small girl no older than six, with a big red bow in her hair.

It is nearly eleven o'clock before the night's entertainment is over, drawn to a close with a picture of George VI projected on the screen and a final rendition of 'God Save the King'. It takes a while for the building to empty: 'I knew they wouldn't have enough exits,' mutters one grumbler. But the chatter is generally positive. It is, as one first-nighter declares, 'absolutely the last word in pictures – it's a Palace'.

4.

Making Ends Meet

After the sparkle of the Odeon opening at the weekend, Monday morning dawns and the town eases back into the normal routines of a working week. Parkinson Street, a small terraced row of thirty-four houses, is home to both Joan, at number 31, and Marion, at number 22. It is not long past five o'clock, and both girls are still sleeping soundly when the quiet of the early morning is broken by a vehicle revving in the distance and the footsteps of a tram driver on his way to work.

Next door to Marion, at number 24, Joseph Chadwick lies awake. Aged seventy-two, he is the street's oldest inhabitant. He used to work as a lamplighter and would once have been the first to stir, out to tend his lamps in a reminder of a pre-electric age. He no longer needs to wake so early but old habits die hard.

Women rouse themselves and attend to the fires in their hearths. One house at a time, cracks of light appear between curtains and smoke trails upwards from chimneys. There is the rattle of a bin lorry and the noise of a man shovelling coal. Milk bottles are left on doorsteps and post is pushed through letterboxes. A baby is crying somewhere and there is the sound of a lavatory being flushed.

Joan hears her next-door neighbour's door bang as he leaves for work. He is a gardener and a gravedigger – so he will describe himself in the 1939 register – and he wants to take advantage of the early light and the warm morning.

Marion is up now and helping her younger sister. She prepares breakfast for them both – she will write about doing this – and gets her ready for school. Their mother is six months' pregnant and glad of her eldest daughter's help. Marion has also been busy knitting baby clothes.

Next is the clatter of clogs as mill workers leave for the eight o'clock shift. One third of the working adults on the street, men and women, are employed in cotton in some capacity. In a couple of years, Marion and Joan will be among them. Parkinson Street itself is sandwiched between mills, as are so many of Bolton's streets.

Those men who are not employed in the mill work mostly in the construction industry, the iron works, the bleachworks and the railway. They leave too, some carrying their lunch in handkerchiefs or paper bags, heads down and readying themselves for the day ahead.

And then the street is full of children heading off to school. They are noisier than the workers and they laugh and jostle. They are more colourful too, the girls with bright dresses and ribbons in their hair. The children split off in different directions, Marion and Joan veering north towards Pikes Lane. Mildred Beswick at number 34 is out cleaning the front windows of her corner shop and she pauses to smile at the children who wave to her.

Aside from Mildred, and Emily Gethings at number 26 who works in a fish and chip shop, those women who aren't employed in cotton are housewives and young mothers. Now they've seen their older children off they attend to their housework. Their children and maybe husbands will be back at noon for their dinner.

Monday is the weekly wash day in Bolton, as in other working-class towns, and the backs of the terraces begin to fill up with the laundry that is pegged out on the washing lines that stretch between the streets. Rows of floating pillowcases, sheets and shirts like these will capture the imagination of Mass Observation's photographer, Humphrey Spender, who makes a special study of them.

Come the afternoon and Parkinson Street is quieter again. A rag and bone man passes through, and then later a window cleaner touting for business. A man is out sweeping his yard, and for a few moments his rhythmic brush strokes are the only sound. If toddlers allow, there might even be time for mothers to sit down and have a cup of tea. The bulk of the washing is done, and the ironing can wait till tomorrow.

The schools empty out and from now on there will be children playing around the houses until dark. It is a part of the day that Joan loves. When Miss Kemp asks her to write an essay on 'money', she will turn up her nose at the 'fine clothes' of the rich, which means that 'they are not allowed to go out unless it is very warm and the children are not allowed to play on summer nights'.

The children tend to congregate in the back streets,

running, skipping, throwing balls, perhaps chalking graffiti on the yards and walls. Earlier in the year, Mass Observation had made a study of children's chalk marks. They record many drawings of heads and faces – executed with varying levels of skill – but also haphazard scrawling, hearts cut through with arrows and, only occasionally, the cruder scribblings of body parts.

The early evening is busy. A few leave for the attractions of the town centre – perhaps even to try out the new Odeon – or for a stroll in nearby Queen's Park. People are popping in and out of the corner shop. The man at number 11 leaves for his weekly trip to the local wrestling stadium, in a converted mill on Turton Street. He is unemployed at the moment, which makes attendance trickier, especially with a young family, but he is the keenest of fans, and for the moment can continue to find the sixpence he needs every Monday for the cheapest standing place. The best thing about it, he tells Mass Observation, is that it teaches self-defence, 'and if I had one hundred children they would all have to watch all-in-wrestling with that one view'.

By about nine o'clock children are starting to be called in and lights begin to be switched off. Mildred Beswick has already shut up her shop and turned the sign around in the window. Activity slows with the fading of the summer light, though from somewhere comes the sound of a man's voice, singing. People slip home and, one by one, the houses darken. By about midnight, everything is quiet.

The longest resident of Parkinson Street is Elizabeth Martindale at number 6. She was just ten years old in 1901 when the census officials made their rounds. She will still be there to be recorded again in 1939, living with her younger sister, both of them working at the cotton mill.

She has known the rhythms of this street for the best part of four decades, joining the daily movement of people to and from school, work and play. She has seen the comings and goings, the friendships and the fallings out.

She has been part of the intimate life of the street but has also seen it touched by the biggest of global events. She was twenty-five when a telegraph boy came down Parkinson Street to deliver the announcement of her brother's death at Bethune, France, in February 1916. Her mother died in 1917, and so was spared the arrival of a second telegram and the death of a second son in September 1918, achingly close to the end of the war.

Elizabeth Martindale has seen other changes too. In 1911, ten Martindales had been living in their four-roomed house, two-up, two-down: eight children aged between three and twenty, with more on the way. By the 1930s this kind of overcrowding is no longer so common. Marion's household of five – Marion, her parents, sister and soon-to-arrive baby brother – is one of the largest families in the street.

It should have been a family of six, of course. Marion's oldest brother had died before she was born. He had been a summer baby and Marion's aunts had been supposed to be looking after him. It had been a hot day and they had left him out in the sun for too long. Her dad could never bring himself to speak to his sisters again.

When, in 1942, Mass Observers asked local people about what changes they would like to see after the war, dozens of them referenced better housing: 'there should be a bath in every house', said one young woman; 'space for a little garden', suggested an older man. The trend towards smaller families may have eased some of the overcrowding that exacerbated poor housing conditions, but many of Bolton's residents continued to live in densely-packed terraced streets, in houses that were cramped, damp and difficult to maintain. On one occasion, Joan fantasised about living somewhere other than Parkinson Street: 'I should have a garden at the front full of rambling roses, forget-me-nots and other dainty looking flowers.'

At the beginning of the 1930s, an investigation by the Bolton Housing Survey Committee had declared many parts of the town to be insanitary. The area to the east of the town – where three-quarters of the houses were almost a hundred years old – was particularly dilapidated. The investigators uncovered overcrowding, a lack of ventilation and defective sanitation. 'The position of many streets and dwellings is such that some houses get practically no sunlight,' they wrote. The district is 'indescribably squalid and depressing'. The conditions, they thought, were to blame for 'a tendency to rickets' and a more general 'lowering of vitality' in the population.

They found walls that were propped up to prevent them from collapse, floors that threatened to give way, roofs that leaked, and damp in whichever direction they looked. A quarter of households had to share toilet facilities; over a quarter suffered vermin infestations from cockroaches, bugs, rats and mice. The investigators were particularly appalled by one house they visited in which a child seriously ill with pneumonia was lying in bed in the kitchen, to be kept company each night by the rats which came through the rotten wall panelling; or another in which 'a stream of liquid from the overflow of defective pails reached to the door of a house and settled there'.

Since then some of the worst slum housing had been cleared under a five-year programme embarked upon by the local council. Around seven hundred of the worst houses had been demolished by 1937. Others were reconditioned and back-to-back houses knocked through to create a single dwelling. The East Ward was a particular focus of these efforts, but some of the streets around Pikes Lane School were also earmarked for clearance, and so its pupils became familiar with a landscape of demolition and rubble, even before the aerial attacks that would follow during the war.

And yet insanitary conditions persisted. Bed bugs continued to be a particular problem and a new disinfecting station was opened in 1937 by the housing department. It specialised in sterilising the belongings of those moving from clearance areas to new corporation housing. Number 85 Davenport Street, the house that Mass Observation rented as its headquarters, was 'crawling', its investigators reported, estimating that 20 per cent of all working-class houses were definitely bug infested, and that was counting only those houses about which 'the owners were ready to admit it'.

When Dr R. M. Galloway, Bolton's Medical Officer of Health, was interviewed by a Mass Observer in 1937, he spoke of houses that were still 'dark, dank and smelling', with a lack of air and proper water supply. Some still had no hot water, bath or inside toilet – even outside toilets might be shared between families. In his official report that year he noted that although progress had been made, a great deal of property in Bolton remained below standard and no fewer than 812 houses had been found to be in a state 'dangerous to health'.

Annie lives in the Pocket, a poor district made up of a handful of streets to the west of Pikes Lane, bounded by the railway to the north and mills to either side. It is an area well known, according to Mass Observation, 'for its poverty, hard living and semi-slum conditions'. Her family have been part of this close-knit community for years, since at least the early 1880s, when the census recorded her grandfather bringing up his young family there. Her father will be working in the mill by the time he's twelve but yearns for adventure and will turn his back on cotton as soon as he is old enough to join the army. He serves in China, India and South Africa before returning to the little corner of the Pocket in 1906, after nearly a decade away; he will stay there for the rest of his life.

His family stay close by too, and Annie grows up at 56 Balshaw Street alongside cousins at both number 60 and 64. Annie's daughter will come here to visit her grandparents when she's small, and will later tell us her memories of the house: of stepping straight off the pavement into a room dominated by a large dresser and the big black range used for cooking, before entering the small back room that contained a pot sink, a single gas ring and a mangle – enormous to a child's eyes – against one wall. The house has no bathroom and, as a child, Annie has to wash in a tin bath in front of the fire. The toilet is in the backyard and she is grateful that, unlike elsewhere in the area, they don't have to share it with other families.

Her father has been back in the mill for many years now and the steady job means that the family can manage. 'Clean, well behaved and neat appearance' is Cawson's assessment of Annie. The family can afford an annual day trip to Blackpool, and every year Annie keeps a grainy photograph of herself taken at the weighing machine. Her 1937 headshot well matches Cawson's description, and she smiles out at the camera. She is almost dead on five stone – very small and slender for a girl just turned thirteen.

Annie is acutely aware of the pressure her parents are under. 'At the weekend when you get the wages you think you can have a good time,' she writes. 'But no, there is the rent, club and other things to pay for. By Monday it is nearly all gone.' You also need money, she explains, to buy 'clothes, shoes and toffees'.

The network of kinship ties is invaluable to families trying to eke out a decent living, and her father and his two brothers can easily keep an eye out for each other, living so close. Support extends to those outside the family too, and the Pocket's warm sense of community will be referenced by other former residents in memoirs written later in the century. When Mass Observation runs a competition about the nature of happiness, many of the entrants say that neighbourliness is important to them. One man, who lives down the street from Annie, explains that 'happiness is sharing life unselfishly'. Annie plays her small part when she takes her neighbour's baby to the cinema.

Some families still find it hard to cope. About a classmate living nearby, Cawson is particularly disparaging: 'Very cheeky and dirty. Very dirty home, no carpets. Mischievous. Carroty hair and red face. Very badly dressed.' Two years later she will be working at the mill, but she fights her destiny nonetheless and tells Miss Kemp that she wants to be a film star when she grows up.

Mary lives in the Pocket too. 'Not at all well off' is Cawson's assessment, and certainly the size of the family makes it harder to make ends meet. By 1937 there are seven children, only two old enough to be earning themselves, and another baby on the way. Mary's father had gone straight to the mill after leaving school, but has worked his way up through hard graft, charm and good fortune. The 1939 register will record him as a 'foreman, sewer works'. He prides himself on being an entrepreneur, and by the 1930s he is unusual in owning – rather than renting – the house they live in, and also works a smallholding with a horse, chickens and pigs. He stables the rag and bone man's pony and, after the war, will rent out garage space to those who own cars.

Mary has to help, of course, and she learns how to make pigswill out of stale bread, how best to spread sawdust on the floor of the pigpens and helps her mother with the washing that she takes in for extra money. Her parents reward her with threepence of pocket money a week; on the day on which she is asked how she spent it she has treated herself to an Aero chocolate bar and put the rest into her money box.

When she is older, Mary, like Annie, will bring her daughter here to visit her elderly parents, and her little girl will love learning all these chores in turn, now recast as treats and special time spent with her grandparents, rather than part of the daily grind of survival.

Those who lived in the poorest housing were often forced to do so because of underlying poverty. Bolton was a town still suffering from the effects of an economic depression that hit the north of England – as well as Wales, Scotland and Northern Ireland – particularly hard. Some of the town's key industries such as cotton, coal and engineering were devastated. Although Bolton did not suffer as badly as its near neighbours Blackburn and Burnley, the 1931 census recorded some 19 per cent of its working men and 13 per cent of its working women as unemployed. When Tom Harrisson first arrived in 1936, scouting out possible locations for future research, he felt that 'the whole *atmosphere* of the place breathed insecurity and dread of unemployment'.

When the Mass Observers talked to people about their lives they heard stories of constant scrimping and daily sacrifice. A woman whose husband had to take time off work through illness told them that she didn't know how they would manage: 'Yesterday it was awful. The kids couldn't understand that there weren't any butties. It's hard when the kids go hungry.' An elderly couple explained that because they possessed just one set of underclothes each, they couldn't go out when these were being washed. Someone else confided that they had had just one day's holiday in fifteen years. A barber reported that 'monies are not freely spent in Bolton, like they are in the south'.

In 1937, benefits paid to the jobless might just about have kept a small family above the poverty line. Where there were more than a couple of children the family would soon fall below it. Older children could help support the family by bringing wages home themselves, of course, but because of the way that benefits were allocated, anything those children earned reduced the amount their father might otherwise be entitled to receive.

It meant that even school-age children were pulled in to help make ends meet. When asked how much spending money she received each week, Jessie claimed a grand sum of more than two shillings, most of it earnt through chores done for a range of neighbours and extended family. She spent it on toffee, ice-cream and stockings, she said, as well as putting some of it away, but she also gave sixpence to her father each week 'as he is not working'.

For the larger families in the class, life could be a struggle even when a parent was employed. Two of the girls in Senior II were sisters – Ada one of the oldest in the class, Peggy one of the youngest. They were middle children in a family of seven and were desperately poor. When Cawson wrote his pen sketch of Ada, he diagnosed possible malnutrition and noted that her beautiful auburn hair had had to be clipped very short, due to a dirty scalp that was covered in sores. She cried to lose it, he wrote. 'How often do you go away?' asked Miss Kemp in a set of written questions to the class. 'I never go away,' answered Ada. 'Where do you go?' was the next question. 'Nowhere.'

Their father was an unemployed miner who had now managed to secure a place at the mill; their mother had to move from Bolton in her search for work – Cawson noted her absence in 1937, and the 1939 register records her as still living away from her family, working at a cotton mill in Farnworth. No doubt she was furiously missing her children even as she knew that this was the best way to provide for them; perhaps she was also guiltily grateful for the time to herself.

In the absence of their mother the two girls shouldered much of the responsibility for the housework. Ada was let out early from school at 11.45 every morning to get dinner ready. She knew how to make 'a proper meal which only costs a few pence which is also a great boon for a large family', as she wrote in one of her school essays.

Peggy was absent from school so often that she contributed only one essay to those collected by Mass Observation, fewer than any other girl in the class. It was an essay entitled 'Money and its uses'; in it she showed that she knew exactly how much her father was bringing home – and it was not a lot. She presumably was already involved in budgeting and counting the pennies at home. 'People work hard to earn this money to pay the rent, coal, clubs and sometimes furniture,' she wrote. 'They work five and a half days to earn about £1 16 8½d per week.'

When all else failed, the threat of the workhouse loomed in the background. Although workhouses were being phased out, having been formally abolished in 1930, in practice they continued to admit those with no other form of support. When a Mass Observer visited Bolton's workhouse, he did not go in. Instead he spoke to some of the men waiting to enter. There were about sixty of them in the queue, all coatless and getting soaked in the heavy rain. It was coming up to Christmas, and he spotted the coloured paper decorations that had been put up in the hallway and around the lamps in an attempt to conjure up a festive atmosphere. Although the men seemed grateful to be admitted, it was unlikely to have been a particularly happy Christmas for them.

In 1937 there were still more than two thousand children within the walls of an English or Welsh workhouse. Destitute, homeless or orphaned children might be sent to other types of institution too, including children's homes and the new approved schools, but it was the workhouse, with its harsh Dickensian undertones, that remained the ultimate symbol of hardship for this generation as for others.

A couple of years earlier, Eliza had been one of those children. Her father had died in April 1933: of broncho-pneumonia, according to the death certificate; of 'softening of the brain' according to Cawson. Whatever the background, it seems that her mother had been unable to cope and had already left the family. Eight-year-old Eliza had been sent to the workhouse with her older sister, to stay there until her mother, distraught, came to claim them.

By 1937 they were living with their mother and her new husband, and Eliza seemed happy. She filled her school essays with news of Blackpool holidays and cinema trips, but the uncertainty of her early years had left its mark. When asked to write on the topic of money, she noted that 'it is very hard to get and without it we could not live', adding that 'the poor people often die through the lack of money for when there is only one man working in a house and there is a family of children one wage does not last long'.

If she was the only girl in the class to have spent time in the workhouse, few Bolton families felt themselves to be beyond its grasp. In 1937 the spectre of pauperism still haunted those who might be only a pay day or two away from destitution. 'I think everybody is about three weeks from the workhouse,' one woman told Mass Observation.

It was this kind of capricious unfairness that informed the girls' moral opinions of money. Elsie had heard that in London, 'urchins run about hungry, barefoot and cold, simply because they have no money to buy their necessities'.

In a very rare reference to formal politics, she also knew that 'in Parliament there are disputes over money which is given in the form of pension to the blind, lame, deaf and many others'.

Most of the girls wouldn't have thought of their opinions as political, but informed by what they saw around them every day. 'Sometimes people who have too much of it like millionaires and other rich people go mad or get very miserly and will not give a copper to the poor,' wrote Mavis, adding that 'the poor people who have no money sometimes are tempted to steal, then money is evil when that happens'. She was careful with the sixpence that she received in pocket money each week. She used some for a weekly trip to the baths and an occasional visit to the pictures but saved the rest. 'I think money should be dealt out better and the rich people get less and the poor more,' she concluded.

Others agreed. 'It is not right that some people should have more than others for it causes trouble and jealousy,' wrote one of her classmates, while another believed that 'the richer people should give the poorer some of their fortune instead of seeing them starve'. It is not, perhaps, surprising that the future wartime message of fair shares and equality of sacrifice fell on such fertile ground. Even before the so-called 'people's war', these girls had firm ideas about how to make the world a better, and a fairer, place.

Parkinson Street survived into the twenty-first century but many of Bolton's other streets did not. The clearing of housing continued after the war and beyond. The Davenport Street house used by Mass Observation as its Bolton base was demolished in the early 1980s. So too were many of the streets around Pikes Lane School, some of which were later to become the location for Bolton University.

Most of the streets that used to make up the Pocket were cleared in the 1960s to make way for a new council estate. Mary moved into one of these new houses and lived there for the rest of her life. It had a backyard and she carefully nurtured a small patch of garden within it. It was hardly the smallholding of her father, but she loved it.

Annie lived at 56 Balshaw Street until she married. Her daughter sketched out the rest of her life for us, according to the houses in which she lived: a small rented two-up two-down on the other side of Bolton as a newly-wed, then back to the area around Pikes Lane when she had children. Later she bought a two-bedroom bungalow in nearby Little Lever, and then a three-bedroom bungalow with a nice garden, which was her final home. 'She was very proud of where she ended up,' her daughter tells us.

Houses mattered. But Annie also knew that happiness was made up of more than material goods. 'Money is very valuable to you when you have none,' she wrote wisely, aged thirteen, but 'when you have plenty of money you are not always happy.'

5.

Church and Chapel

Every Sunday Annie attends the Pocket Mission at the end of her street. It is an outpost of the Saviour's Church, which is one of the largest religious buildings in Bolton and just over the other side of the main road, but Church and Mission cater for two different types of worshipper.

The Saviour's itself is hardly exclusive. 'We have no rich people here,' one of its church wardens tells Joe Wilcock, a Mass Observer – himself a lay preacher – who has been tasked with leading the team's investigation into the religious life of the town. A few of the Pikes Lane girls are members of the Church, including Joan, who writes about the egg and flower Sunday school service she goes to on Easter Day. She surely knows the vicar's daughter, who is a few classes below Senior II, in the school's junior department. Years later, in 1949, Joan will also marry here; her marriage certificate records her as living at 31 Parkinson Street until then.

But the warden admits to Wilcock that the very poorest

don't want to attend the Church: 'They prefer to go in their shawls to the Mission.' The Saviour's has carpeting, red hassocks to kneel on, wrought-iron chandeliers and electric lighting. It can hold eight hundred people when full. The Pocket Mission is held in a single room, created by knocking two terraced houses together. It's a sparsely furnished space, with cream walls, bare floorboards and a whitewashed ceiling. On a platform at one end, a lectern and three chairs are placed on a threadbare carpet. Alongside sits an organ, looking rather the worse for wear.

The Mission is for those who 'feel out of place amidst the respectability and orderliness of the parish church', writes Wilcock. But if the Mission reflects the poverty of its members, then the spirit of the place goes some way to making up for it. The atmosphere is 'very homely and inclusive', he reports, though he also notes that services are sometimes interrupted by boys throwing bricks against the door.

The vicar rarely visits, and his curate has never been seen at a Mission service. A Church Army sister oversees the day-to-day business. She is acutely aware of the social conditions that affect those who attend and refuses to accept that nothing can be done. Today her address tackles the theme of slum clearance; sometimes she talks about the need for a fairer social system or the abolition of poverty. The congregation bend their heads in worship, and she leads the prayers for a better life ahead.

Annie likes the hymns best, and the way the noise fills the room. She always sings her heart out. She'll do the same in her old age, when she sits in front of the TV and watches *Songs of Praise*.

*

Sunday was different to other days in Bolton. Even mothers might get the chance to relax a bit. Games were forbidden in the parks, and the art gallery, library and most shops were closed. So too were the cinemas; in fact, Bolton was to hold out against Sunday cinema opening longer than most English towns. 'Sunday is God's gift; would you misuse any priceless gift given to you by your father?' asked a sign outside a Methodist church. It was an unsuitable metaphor, thought the Mass Observer who jotted it down, given that few Bolton parents could afford costly presents.

The streets are empty of the usual noise and traffic. Buses and trams won't start running until the afternoon. Instead, the chiming of bells rings out across the town as church after church call their congregations to prayer. The patchwork of sound impresses the Mass Observers sufficiently that they start questioning passers-by: 'Do they notice this bell-ringing or is it so much a part of their lives that they think of it no more than breathing?' they wonder.

'Are you a stranger here? Don't they ring in every town?' is one surprised response. Others are more hostile: 'They get on your nerves', 'a bloody nuisance'. In a fish and chip shop in the centre of town the proprietor is upset at recent proposals to stop the sale of fish and chips on a Sunday. 'If they want to stop something on Sundays why don't they stop church bell ringing?' he complains. A customer agrees, muttering something about wringing necks instead of bells.

'Do the bells make you want to go to church?' an Observer asks a youngish man who he has stopped in the street. 'Yes,' the man replies. 'Many a time.' In fact, he'd left the house early that morning with exactly that intention, but the bright winter sunshine had seduced him, and he'd decided to take a walk instead.

For those more determined to mark the day as holy, there is no shortage of places to worship. Bolton is home to forty-one religious denominations that meet in over one hundred and fifty different churches and chapels, plus one synagogue. There are around forty Anglican churches and sixteen Roman Catholic ones, according to Mass Observation's rough estimates, but Bolton's religious life is dominated by its strong nonconformist tradition. At school, the girls are taught of the town's history as a Puritan and Parliamentary stronghold during the Civil War – a 'Geneva of the North'. They learn that the massacre of Bolton's soldiers and citizens that followed the Royalist takeover in 1644 was one of the worst atrocities of that war.

By the 1930s, there are dozens of Methodist churches. Some of the venues are enormous: the Bolton Methodist Mission's Victoria Hall, which opened in 1900, was designed in the style of a music hall with 1,250 tiered seats in both a main hall and gallery; the King's Hall opened a few years later on a similar model. They exist alongside numerous smaller sects such as the Mazdaznan, Beulah, Bethel and Advent: 'small but moderately successful', according to Mass Observation, 'tremendously intense, utterly anti-pub, anti-alcohol'.

Marion belongs to the Salvation Army. She goes twice a day on Sundays, she tells Miss Kemp, upping it on Easter Sunday to 'morning, afternoon and night'. On Easter Monday she goes to Liverpool to watch her cousins take part in a Salvationist concert. 'It was lovely,' she reports. 'As we were going for the train we went to look at the water and to see the ships go out.'

Marion herself is surely in the procession around Bolton that Tom Harrisson observes a few weeks later; a larger affair than usual with bands travelling from elsewhere in Lancashire to attend. Almost everyone is in uniform and the girls wear red, white or blue sashes. 'There's music in the Heart where Jesus dwells' proclaims the banner on a lorry that comes trundling past. Eight girls sit in tableau wearing long dresses and bands round their hair, labelled joy (pale blue), admiration (yellow), hate (deep blue), grief (black), horror (red), scorn (green) and love (white). 'Hate' is the oldest girl. 'She looks sulky, as if she hates it,' Harrisson comments.

But onlookers seem to enjoy it. 'Smiles are the most common on people's faces,' says Wilcock, of another Salvation Army parade. 'A man, perhaps the owner of the tobacco shop near to the corner comes to the door and stands there, although this band must have been along this street for years, the Hall is only round the corner, and they are out every Sunday night.'

As far as we know, Marion is the only member of the Salvationists among the girls of Senior II, but several of her classmates, including Mary, belong to the Hebron Hall. Established before the war, its worshippers meet in a long, squat building, a few streets further down Deane Road from Pikes Lane, and are offered an austere form of worship. 'It is a pretty strict place,' writes Miss Kemp. 'No pictures or dancing.' Members pass through a dark vestibule into a simple, square-shaped room with a raised reading desk draped in brown velvet cloth, ringed with benches.

There are no decorations or flowers. Texts painted on the walls exclaim, 'By grace are ye saved through faith'; 'Unto you we believe he is precious' and 'Jesus Christ the same yesterday and today and forever'.

Another asks, 'What think ye of Jesus?' It is a question that Mary has already answered at school, as the topic of one of the essays that Miss Kemp sets the class. He is 'a good and honest and very clever man', Mary decides, who 'did good for everybody'. She adds, 'If a leper was coming down the street he would go up to him and clean him.' 'He is kind of a gentle and good fellow, always waiting for little boys and girls to believe in him,' writes another of the Hebron Hall girls.

It is not the only religious question that Miss Kemp poses to her pupils, and on separate occasions she also asks them to put down their thoughts on Heaven and Hell. Mass Observation might well have asked her directly to do this: a book on religious life in Bolton is one of the researchers' priorities, although in the end they never manage to complete it.

The girls got at least some of their knowledge of scripture from their lessons at Pikes Lane. It is hard to know exactly what they were taught, though they'd evidently just been learning about the Conversion of Saul when they wrote their essays about Jesus. A few of the children forgot to start a new page as instructed, and their final sentences about Paul fill the space above.

They also received their religious education from their Sunday school. If active and regular churchgoing was a minority pursuit among Bolton adults, Sunday school was near universal among its children. When asked whether or not they went, only three of the forty-one girls in the class – one of them Molly – said that they didn't. Children were sent even when their parents' attendance had slipped, not least because it offered a form of childcare. As Madge explained, 'I do not go for the sake of a prize, it's to keep me out of the streets.'

Sunday School activities included hymns, readings and talks, perhaps on the evils of drink or gambling. Several of the girls mentioned their Sunday school when they wrote of their Easter holiday activities. Another of the Saviour's girls had learnt that 'Judas Iscariot sold Jesus for fifty pieces of silver, and he was captured in the garden of Gethsemane.'

The quality of teaching was, of course, variable. In the summer, one unnamed Mass Observer sat in on a Sunday school session at the Saviour's Church, held in a big room behind the main church building. Joan was on the roll, having not yet reached her thirteenth birthday, after which she would move up to the senior class. The superintendent was a small woman, soberly dressed, who struggled to keep order. There were around one hundred children in the room, aged between seven and twelve, and they were rowdy. One or two 'uncontrollables' raced about as though it were a playground. She tried to shout above the din, resorting to pleading or threats, both of which were ineffective.

The session started with a hymn and the children became reasonably quiet for prayers, though 'it can hardly be said that the atmosphere is prayerful. They will put their hands together but it is much more difficult for them to close their eyes.' Then the children moved to separate parts of the hall into a dozen different groups separated by age and sex.

Most of the teachers were in their early twenties, four of them men, the majority women. They were 'an amiable crowd' but demonstrated little co-ordination and even less efficiency, wrote the Observer. Commitment was also variable: Sunday school teachers had been seen manicuring their nails during hymns and prayers; somebody once left to go to a different Sunday school just so she could join its hockey team.

The girls surely paid some attention to their religious lessons nonetheless, whether delivered at Pikes Lane, Sunday school or around the dinner table at home. When asked to describe Jesus, they conjured up a good and kind man who healed the sick and died on a cross. Their descriptions of Heaven drew on standard tropes. It was 'a glorious place', 'a place of paradise', with angels fluttering about or playing golden harps, surrounded by stars, flowers, masses of clouds and 'trees bearing golden fruit'. Hell, on the other hand, was 'a dreadful, dark, dismal place' with burning fires and a Devil with a fork 'which he pokes us with'. You are 'watched by crafty looking faces', added Joan.

Lots of the girls put in their own individual embellish-ments. Marion imagined being in Heaven and looking back down at the earth: 'We should be able to see how the rain falls and the snow and the thunder. We would be able to see everybody and what our mother and father, sister, brother, daughter and son was doing.' She was not the only one to mention the weather, and another of her classmates also thought Heaven might offer an escape from the Lancashire climate: 'You do not get wet and the wind does not blow you.'

Some gave very detailed responses. 'There is a running stream near a wall, the devil cuts their heads over the stream and the blood runs in and he lets the head go in and he burns them and they walk about with no heads on,' said Nellie. Joyce D was characteristically thoughtful. 'Some people think it's nice believing in Hell and we think it is nice to believe in Heaven. We just mock them who believe in Hell but perhaps those who believe in Hell may mock us for believing in Heaven.'

A few of the girls were even more sceptical. After providing a particularly dark description of 'a place of fire where wicked people's souls are burnt away to nothing', Irene added that 'I do not think Hell is true'. Molly, one of those who did not attend a Sunday school, was scathing: 'I believe Hell is no place at all only rubbish. A lot of people say it is a big fire where you go if you are naughty and the devil gets hold of you with a fork and pushes you in. I don't believe there is such a place and I do not believe in the devil or the fire they throw you in.'

Alice thought Hell was an imaginary land too, though she had a go at describing it, nonetheless. Satan, horned and dressed in red, sits on a throne cut into the rock, next to a large fire with 'all funny creatures dancing round', she suggested. But her rejection of Hell was due to her faith in the kindness of her God. 'Jesus died for us,' she wrote.

Alice is a member of the King's Hall Methodist Mission, one of the two big Methodist halls. She belongs to a girls' club four hundred-strong, while the Boys' Brigade boasts another one hundred members. Both play their part 'in the making of sober citizens', a mill owner tells Mass Observation.

In April, a girls' group from the King's Hall perform 'A Biblical Play' based on the life of Jesus, with proceeds going towards the missionary weekend. The actors are aged between nine and twenty, but the Mass Observer present makes no concessions for their youth. 'The whole thing is crudely amateurish,' he writes, detailing a litany of errors: the small children who neglect to face the audience and can't be heard; the excited children who give their lines before they are even fully onto the stage; the nervous children who forget their lines altogether. He takes exception to Joseph in particular, 'played by an elderly girl, in a bit of a soprano voice, not in the least masculine'. Finally, the costumes: 'in my opinion more Bedouin than Jewish'.

'The whole thing is unutterably boring,' he concludes. 'Still, it seemed to be what the people liked.' Afterwards he notices the actors talking to members of the audience. Those coming to watch must be relatives, he thinks, here out of loyalty.

We don't know whether or not Alice took part in this particular play, though we do know that she liked acting; we have a photo of her from 1936, in costume as Boy Blue: 'The day I was the principal boy', she has written on the back in her eleven-year-old handwriting. She is talented too, certainly a good dancer – 'won first prize', writes Cawson in his pen sketch.

But whether she was in the play, in the audience or sat this one out, such events demonstrated the efforts made by the churches to provide a community that went beyond a weekly Sunday service. A regular Saturday night concert was a tradition at both the Methodist halls, ostensibly for entertainment but also a useful opportunity to spread the Christian message. At another event at the King's Hall, the parson ended the evening by announcing that he 'hopes everyone will go to bed early and that there will be a good congregation in the morning'. Admission was twopence, set deliberately low 'to attract the poorest and the young'.

The Mass Observer Brian Barefoot attends one of the Saturday concerts at the Victoria Hall in mid-September, one of an audience of about 650 people who fill the ground floor; the balcony is closed off. The vast majority are women, although there are a few dozen children present too. The concert is a more professional one this time, but he is not impressed. Perhaps those in attendance have already been to the pictures that week; perhaps they don't like pubs, he thinks – a large number must be church members, 'but church loyalty would not be sufficient to explain the presence of so many people at a show which was inferior to almost any cinema show'.

Barefoot settles back in his seat to watch. The performers have come from nearby Burnley, and he lists the various acts: drinking songs, patriotic songs, a song about a swallow, another about a clock. A man performs the Toreador song from *Carmen*, and the hall echoes with it as people whistle along or tap their shoes in time. There are some dramatic sketches: some serious Dickensian monologues; a comic sketch of a man trying to quiet a wailing baby, which gets roars of laughter. A silent film completes the evening, projected onto a roll of white cloth. Barefoot doesn't think much of it – 'very antiquated and badly produced' – but those around him seem to enjoy it.

In between the acts, the minister gives an address on the harvest festival. The Rev. Hannah is a fine orator, 'a good spell-binder', talking very sincerely and using his hands and arms to great effect, another Mass Observer had noted on a different occasion, but this evening Barefoot is more interested in the reactions of the audience, who titter at some of the mentions of different fruit and vegetables. He lists their 'order of humorousness': bananas, which get the biggest laugh, then potatoes, tomatoes, grapes, flowers. No one laughs at flowers. 'Is it the repetition of syllables that is amusing?' he wonders.

Possibly in the audience that night, and certainly a member of the Victoria Hall Mission, is a boy called Roland, the same age as Alice. The youth groups of the two mission halls often meet up, and Alice and Roland might already know each other. By the time they're sixteen they are childhood sweethearts.

His parents won't approve of the match and will refuse to sanction talk of marriage. They pride themselves on being a family with standing: both are teachers and Roland joins the bank when he leaves school. Alice, on the other hand, is illegitimate and her mother only a weaver. Besides, the pair are both so young.

But Roland is besotted and won't give up. The courtship continues during the war. Roland joins the army, proves himself to be an exceptional marksman, and spends the war in relative safety in Britain, training new recruits. He turns twenty-one in April 1945, and four months later – parental approval no longer needed – he marries Alice.

The faith that brought them together will stay strong for the rest of their lives, although Alice eventually follows Roland into Quakerism. They will celebrate their blue sapphire wedding anniversary at the Quaker Meeting House, sixty-five years later.

6.

Family

On the Thursday before Easter, Alice sets out with her mother Lily for their regular trip to Glazebury to visit Alice's aunt. It's a long journey – a forty-minute walk out of Bolton to Four Lane Ends, a half-hour bus ride from there to Leigh, and then another hour on foot. They make the trip most weeks, usually there and back in a day, but this time they're staying over for Easter. It will be a squeeze in the tiny house, but Alice is glad for the break in the journey. She and her mum are frozen through when they arrive that night, and the next morning there will be snow on the ground.

Auntie Annie is glad of her sister's help. She is disabled and finds it difficult to get around. Her husband died of cancer years ago and, although her two sons are good to her, it's not the same as having other women around to help. Both boys are busy with their own lives, and her eldest, Billy, is married now with a baby on the way.

The little village of Glazebury is in the middle of nowhere, or so it seems to Bolton-bred Alice, and her cousins are proper country men. Both are fond of their little cousin and she enjoys their attention, getting up willingly in the mornings to help Walter feed the chickens. He takes her on a long country yomp on the Saturday and drills her – as is his habit – on the flowers, trees and birds. She's already got a reputation at school for being good at nature study, the one who knows the names for everything. She'll lose interest when she's older, but for now she laps it up. 'We saw the brown linnet', she writes in her essay about the trip when she gets back to the classroom the following week.

Several years older than her, Billy and Walter go some way to replacing the father Alice doesn't have. When, a few years later, Roland signs up for the army, it is to cousin Billy that he writes to ask if he will take care of his Alice should anything happen to him. Nothing does, and when they marry in 1945 it is cousin Walter who gives Alice away.

Family mattered in 1930s Britain. Relatives could usually be relied on to help each other out when times were tough, and the expectation of mutual aid was widely shared. Aunts featured prominently in the lives of the Pikes Lane girls, whether as companions on outings, providers of treats, or sources of pocket money, usually in return for errands. Cousins provided playmates – for Molly, they went some way to compensating for her lack of siblings – and several of the girls minded younger cousins in the same way that they might look after smaller brothers or sisters, just as they might once have been minded by older cousins in turn.

As Alice's trips out to Glazebury showed, relationships

with extended family could be built into weekly schedules, with social visits, chores and obligations threaded through the year. Irene spent Good Friday visiting her cousin who lived out in the countryside. Their house had a garden, which – to Irene's delight – was home to several rabbits, and an attic with 'plush chairs' and an electric fire, which was used as a playroom. Irene enjoyed herself hugely but also felt slightly envious, writing later about how many toys her cousin had to play with. 'I was very sorry when I had to go home.'

But when Miss Kemp asked her pupils to write about home and family, the person they mentioned most often was their mother.

Alice was particularly close to her mother Lily. Even Cawson noticed. 'Great pals with mother. Go about together,' he wrote. Lily had been born in Bolton, the youngest of seven sisters, a few months into the new century. Three sisters had died before she was really able to remember them: fifteen-year-old Mary in 1902; eight-year-old Eveline in 1903; nineteen-year-old Ellen in 1904. The family were poor, and the girls had been able to mount little defence when disease struck. By the time Lily was fifteen her mother had died too. Her father coped by turning to drink. The sisters coped by holding each other together.

Another decade later, and Lily will be knocking at Alice's father's house to tell him that she is pregnant. His mother answers the door and tells her to get packing. It is rumoured that he leaves the country soon after. Lily will take his name to the grave with her; however many times Alice asks, she will never tell.

But Lily already knows the strength of female kinship.

When Alice is born the sisters extend the protective circle around the new baby. 'Aunts take great interest,' writes Cawson, thirteen years later. Mother and daughter move around – at one point they are living in the Pocket – but in 1937 they share a little house in Hawthorne Street. It has the luxury of the tiniest of hallways, lined with coat pegs, on which Lily hangs a man's coat so no stranger might think that she is there with her daughter alone.

There are a small number of girls whose mothers are absent, either living apart or deceased – and here grandmothers often step in – but mothers remain central to the lives of most. Not all are lucky enough to share the closeness of Alice and Lily, although another classmate enjoys playing cards with her mother every night. But for many of the girls, the experiences they share with their mother are rooted in the day-to-day of household chores, and this is what they write about.

When Miss Kemp tidies the classroom at the end of one school day, she keeps an eye on the handful of girls who have been asked to stay behind to finish their spellings. One of them has been sneaking glances at the clock for a while now and can't contain herself any longer. 'Oh look, it's half past four and on Thursday I mop the pantry,' she tells her teacher hopefully.

'Do you have to do a lot of housework?' asks Miss Kemp. 'Yes,' is the reply. 'I wash up after every meal and I mop quite a lot.' Other children join in. 'I help my mother and do a lot of mopping!' says one. 'Of course you should help your mother – what do you think you are on earth for?' says another.

Miss Kemp gives them a smile to show that she concedes, and the girls take their cue and disappear off down the passage, giggling as they go.

'When we are at home we go errands and mop the kitchen and clean windows,' explains Joyce H, another of Senior II's Joyces. She is one of the older girls in the class, thirteen and a half when she writes this in the summer of 1937. She is a very quiet child, according to Cawson, possibly because she has often struggled with poor health. 'Nerve trouble,' he says.

Thanks to her mother, Ellen, Joyce is already a skilled domestic worker. She knows how to mind the house when her mother goes out. She can keep the home tidy, she can lay the fire, and she can cook for the whole family, making sure to clean the pots well should they have been used for anything fatty 'so that it won't leave any mark'. She knows that she sometimes ends up doing jobs that her mother doesn't want to do, but she doesn't seem to mind: 'If our mothers do not like climbing a ladder we should clean the windows and learn not to be giddy on the ladder so we will not fall off.'

She is also a talented needlewoman, dedicating what spare time she has to her embroidery. She thinks that she'd like to be a dressmaker when she grows up, 'so that I will be able to make my own clothes. It is a very useful job.'

Ellen gives her daughter a few pence a week for the work she does in the home and the errands that she runs, and Joyce puts it carefully away in her money box rather than spending it on cinema tickets or sweets like most of her classmates. To make her way as a dressmaker, 'I should have to go to a sewing class for training, and start by doing handkerchiefs on the machine and then doing gathers,' she writes. Perhaps she is already thinking about how she will pay for it.

In fact, Joyce will go straight into the mill when she leaves school six months later, and the 1939 register records her as a quilt weaver. She gives it up when she marries, though will have to take up evening shifts again once her youngest has started at school. Arthritis in her mid-fifties will finally force her to stop for good.

She will never lose her interest in dressmaking though. Her daughter tells us that 'all her life she'd be sewing', making tutus and ballet shoes for her children and, later, grandchildren. When the first great-grandchild comes along, Joyce's fingers will still be nimble enough to make a beautiful, shimmering shawl for the baby. She was always, according to her daughter, 'very happy in the home'.

Girls growing up in the 1930s were expected to help out. Domestic work was hard, despite the new technologies that claimed to save both labour and time. Keeping houses clean and families fed was a particular struggle in Lancashire, a region in which an unusually high proportion of married women were in industrial employment, a fact sometimes blamed for one of the highest rates of maternal mortality in the country. One Bolton housewife told Mass Observation that she had no time for a hobby, 'unless it's doing my mending, sewing'.

When the social reformer Margery Spring Rice researched the lives of married women in this period, she found that many were ill and exhausted with overwork, with little time to themselves. And so the help of their daughters was invaluable, with the girls able to ease the pressure and sometimes take over altogether. 'If mother is ill we learn how to look after her and go her errands,' wrote Marion, while one of her classmates also knew to help out: 'When my mother is ill I can do all the cooking and can get the tea ready for my father.'

Jessie's mother was often unwell. She worked in the cardroom at the mill, a dirty, dusty, noisy job. When asked to describe what she did on her Ascension Day holiday, Jessie confided that, 'My part is not very exciting because my mother being ill and father being out I had to do housework. I had a very miserable night. Staying in plaiting hair-bands is very uncomfortable, but it is what I had to do.'

The girls' training in domestic work started early. Even the nine-year-old girls in a Pikes Lane junior class knew how to wash, bake, iron, mop and sew. 'I like to help mother,' wrote one. 'It is nice to do a little bit of work.' Another girl was even impatient to do more: 'My mother said I could mop the back step when I am ten.' By the time they had graduated to the senior classes these children would have learnt how to do most of the basic tasks that made up the running of a home.

When Miss Kemp asked Senior II about their household chores they could therefore reply in some detail. Madge had an elaborate routine for polishing the linoleum and would get on with the dusting with a feather brush while waiting for the polish to sink in. She knew better than to waste time, for 'there is plenty to be done'. Another girl wrote about beating carpets and mopping flagstones. She could keep the front step nice, dipping a soft donkey stone into a bucket of warm water and rubbing the step until it was covered with a creamy paste to be polished up with a damp cloth. Her friend cleaned the fireplace by getting 'a duster and a packet of black lead and mixing it with cold water. I also get a brush.'

Dora knew how to darn and crochet and 'which way to sweep the carpet because if one has a carpet with flowers it makes the flowers look nicer'. She was also taught how to arrange and clean the furniture in 'the special part of the house'. Her mother's insistence on a faultlessly clean home – even in the rarely used parlour – influenced her daughter's description of Heaven and Hell. 'Heaven has beautiful castles, houses that are spotlessly clean and pavements as white as snow,' wrote Dora, unlike Hell, whose pavements 'are sick with dirt for want of mopping'.

If the girls wondered why their brothers were not expected to help in the same way, they didn't mention it in their essays, although the division of housework sometimes led to tensions between sisters. Mary was continually getting into arguments with her younger sister, who had a talent for finding ways to avoid domestic tasks. Heaven is 'a place where you can't fall out because you have to go errands and wash up, because there is none to do', she imagined, reflecting her frustration.

If the girls of Senior II were adept at washing, polishing, dusting and mopping, then the other skill they needed to know was how to cook. The curriculum at Pikes Lane included fortnightly lessons but most learnt more from their mothers. 'We only cook a small quantity of ingredients when we are at cookery,' explained one girl, 'but I am beginning to know how to cook for large numbers of people.' She was a middle child, with a brother either side, and boasted that her mother was a particularly accomplished baker. 'She is teaching me how to be the same,' she wrote, adding, 'When I grow up I hope to become an excellent woman and a good housewife.'

The girls recorded their culinary lessons with a sense of pride. 'In the afternoon I peeled the potatoes for a potato pie,' said another. 'My mother told me what to do with the meat. Later in the afternoon I made the crust and put it on the pie and at tea-time it turned out very nice.'

Later, when the girls are bringing up their own families, the provision of food becomes a different source of pride. When their sons and daughters later tell us their memories of their mothers, talking about food becomes a way of talking about love and care. The daughters of both the Pocket girls – Mary and Annie – tell us that, however difficult it was for their mothers to make ends meet, 'there was always good food on the table'.

Mary's daughter felt particularly lucky. When she left school, Mary had started work in the kitchens of one of Bolton's convalescent hospitals and had been promoted to head cook by the time she was twenty-one. It was a live-in position, which for Mary was a welcome relief from the chaos and noise of her crowded home. She would later talk about these years as some of the happiest of her life. For her children, it would mean that cheap, nutritious and tasty food was always a given.

In her elder years she relaxed into a grandmother's role, handing out home-made treats instead. Her grandchildren, and later her great-grandchildren, called her 'Nanna Biscuit'.

Mass Observation did extensive research into the household budgets and eating habits of the Bolton townspeople, asking them to record their meals over a week. They found that a pot of tea accompanied everything, as did a plate of bread and butter, and that the main meal was enjoyed at midday – the northern 'dinner' time – with a lighter tea later on. Supper was a snack or perhaps, as a treat, a chip butty crafted out of a soft round barm cake – Lancashire's version of a bread roll. Sunday roasts were a weekly fixture in those households that could afford a joint of meat.

Not content to read about the town's eating habits, some of the investigators also ate with them. Walter Hood was one of Mass Observation's working-class recruits, having grown up in a Durham mining community. He joined a family of five for tea, arriving to find a table packed with 'green salad, trifle, cold meat, and pickles', as well as 'custards, rhubarb tart, sweet cakes and three kinds of plate pies'. The table was so heavily laden that the bread board had to be carefully balanced on top of the sugar bowl. One of several apples sitting on the sideboard looked suspiciously like it had already been bitten into.

Hood politely took just a little of the cold meat and salad, though his hosts urged more food upon him. Their children had no such restraint, and dived in. One of the little girls took advantage of his presence to pick out the egg yolks from the salad, knowing that she wouldn't be reprimanded with a guest at the table. She wolfed down eight of them, Hood observed, and then complained that she didn't feel well.

It seems likely that a visit from a Mass Observer meant that this meal was anything but ordinary – and the children's

When I grow up I should like to be a teacher, because I like teaching & marking books.

Above: No doubt inspired by Miss Kemp, Molly muses on her future.
© *Mass Observation*

Middle: Pikes Lane Elementary School, later knocked down to be replaced by new premises.
© *Bolton News*

Left: Molly.
Photo courtesy of Pat Gallagher

Above: Marion (*left*, *photo courtesy of Brenda Mullineux*) and Joan (*right*, *photo courtesy of Stephen Kenyon*), both of whom lived on Parkinson Street.

Below: A typical Bolton street scene which would have been familiar to all of the girls from Pikes Lane. *© Bolton Council*

at if I should have a garden at the front full of Rambling Roses, forget me Nots, and other dainty looking flowers.

A dreamy extract from one of Joan's essays (*above,* © *Mass Observation*). But many of the girls at Pikes Lane would lead a less romantic life. When workers left the mill at the end of their shift (*middle,* © *Bolton Council*), they would have their domestic chores to attend to (*below,* © *Bolton Council*).

Left: Alice as a young actor playing the part of little boy blue.

Photo courtesy of Margaret R. Marks and J. Olwyn Padidar

Right: Alice celebrating her wedding day in 1945, with her cousin Walter by her side.

Photo courtesy of Margaret R. Marks and J. Olwyn Padidar

Below: An extract from Alice's writing on the Girl Guides camp which she attended.

© *Mass Observation*

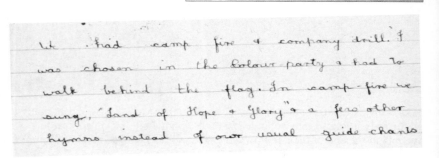

We had camp fire & company drill. I was chosen in the Colour party & had to walk behind the flag. In camp-fire we sung, "Land of Hope & Glory" & a few other hymns instead of our usual guide chants

Alice's mother Lily (wearing dark apron), alongside her fellow millworkers. 'Best mother ever', wrote Alice on the back. *Photo courtesy of Margaret R. Marks and A Olsson Radid.*

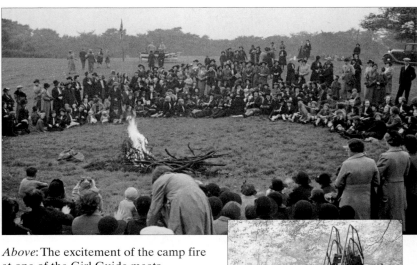

Above: The excitement of the camp fire at one of the Girl Guide meets.
© *Bolton Council*

Right: This rather daunting slide could be found in Queen's Park where many of the girls spent their spare time.
© *Bolton Council*

Below: A group of children pass the time with a game of rounders. Bolton Royal Infirmary is in the background.
© *Bolton Council*

Left: The ever-reliable Woolworths, popular amongst locals and a crucial observation point for the Mass Observation team. © *Bolton Council*

Middle: Bolton's milk bar. © *Bolton Council*

Below: An extract from an essay written by Irene, dwelling on an afternoon well spent. © *Mass Observation*

afternoon. First we went in down, the Market Hall and I had a bottle of milk from the Milk Bar. When we came out we went to Woolworth

Left: Mass Observers Tom Harrisson (*left*) and Walter Hood (*right*), in their rough-and-ready headquarters at 85 Davenport Street.

Below: The Pikes Lane girls.

reaction suggests the same. But the Pikes Lane girls did write about family occasions at which the tables were overladen with tasty items. Mary's eldest sister turned twenty-one at Easter, and the family had celebrated with jelly, custard, coconut macaroons, cream, iced cakes, pears, peaches and home-made cake.

Certainly, when asked to list their favourite foods, the girls could conjure up a range of different treats: treacle cake, bananas and biscuits for Madge; turkey, steak puddings, and potato pie for Marion; sardines, strawberries and chicken for Irene; chicken, ham and eggs, and roast pork for Alice.

Mothers are not the only teachers, even if they are the most frequent ones. Fathers might also train their daughters in a range of skills: how to make table mats out of cork, or how to keep the coal shed clean. Nellie's father – whom she adores – teaches her how to make a rabbit hutch, how to put hinges onto new cupboards, and how to oil bicycles.

Madge's father keeps chickens, as do many Bolton families – indeed when the writer J. B. Priestley passed through, he observed that 'the whole of Lancashire appeared to be keeping poultry'. 'Saturday was an enormous thrill,' Madge writes, about a weekend spent helping her dad. Together they had fed the birds with pocketsful of cabbage leaves, until the cocks had begun to chase her. She had shrieked and run away, dropping the leaves behind her. But she isn't really afraid and goes back a couple of days later to collect the eggs. 'I brought them home and sold them,' she writes proudly – one shilling and threepence per dozen. She is good at drumming up business – 'they are cheap!' she tells passers-by – and they're sold out within fifteen minutes.

Other family members move in and out of the girls' lives as playmates, advisers and co-conspirators – and sometimes as responsibilities too. Those who have younger siblings are often asked to take care of them: 'If mother is busy and she has a baby we learn how to nurse it.' This doesn't always have to feel like a chore – as the Ascension Day holiday drew to an end, one girl 'took the baby to bed with me and that is the end of a perfect day'.

Older siblings – already making their way in the world of work – share their experiences and skills. A brother shows his sister how to loop knots over her fingers, though even after practising she still can't do it as well as him: 'He just throws it over his finger and then he keeps doing it until he has filled his finger with the string.' Another's brother teaches her how to collect birds' eggs from nests.

Older sisters are a source of a different kind of knowledge, advising on which dress to wear or promising a demonstration on how to apply lipstick. At Easter, Dora's sister brings her a very special Easter egg as a present: 'It was not chocolate. It was a round bottle of scent in an egg cup. I thanked her for it and put some on her dress to show my gratitude.'

When Mass Observation ran its competition in Bolton on the nature of happiness, the respondents mentioned family over and over again. 'What would my home be without the occupants?' wrote a young mother. 'What use would money be without companionship? What use would my birthday be with nobody to remember it?'

Another answer came from a Bolton miner, also with small children, whose reply was a love letter to his family. 'When I come home from the pit and see my kiddies and wife I am happy,' he explained. 'When I am washed and romp with my eldest boy I am happy. When it is weekend and I tip up my humble wage and share with my wife in doling it out, and we find we can manage for another week we are happy. I sometimes go for a walk with the wife and children and it makes me happy to see the wife's face and the delight of my eldest boy. I love my home and family, and remember it is not the house that makes the home, it is the love and happiness inside.'

As for Alice, the bond with her mother remained tight for the rest of their lives. We have a photograph of Lily taken in the mill where she worked as a weaver, with the decorations for George V's 1935 jubilee celebrations in the background. 'My mother is in black apron', Alice has written, much later, in adult handwriting on the back. 'Best mother ever'.

She was a wonderful grandmother too, Alice's daughters tell us. They talk about the house in Hawthorne Street, where Alice was living in 1937 and where Lily lived until she died. They remember the smell of the cedarwood drawers, the taste of Blue Riband biscuits and Dandelion and Burdock, and the jar of loose sixpences that was split between the two of them every year.

When it gets dark their nanna puts their pyjamas in the oven next to the fire to warm them up and opens the back door. The ground drops away here and they have a view across the whole of the town, lights flickering in thousands of windows. She puts her arms around them, just like she used to do with Alice, and whispers to them that it's as good as the Blackpool illuminations.

7.

Spare Time

As she does every Thursday evening, Alice changes into a smart uniform of blue blouse and skirt, loosely ties her neckerchief, and heads off to the weekly Girl Guides meeting. It is held in a gymnasium at the back of the Victoria Hall; the Brownies class, which starts a little earlier, is already in progress when she arrives. Several small girls are sitting in a circle on the floor around a number of objects, playing a memory game: they close their eyes and one item is removed, and they then have to say what's missing.

Alice smiles as she remembers doing the same, but steps past them, beyond the screen that divides the hall in two and separates out the older girls. There are eighteen Guides here today, mostly around her age, although girls are welcome until the age of sixteen.

After paying their subs, the girls split up into different patrols and head to separate corners of the room. The members of Swallow patrol rummage through a box of photographs of the Royal Family – they are proud, of course, that Princess Elizabeth herself has recently joined the First Buckingham Palace Guide Company. Those in Thrush patrol are busy tying ropes into various different types of knots, while Poppy corner are learning how to signal with a flag.

The two company leaders are women in their early twenties, dressed in similar uniforms to the girls, with the addition of blue hats. They explain to a Mass Observer present – Joe Wilcock, who surely stands out – that they are there to teach the girls 'instruction in useful arts, and how to look after themselves in the home and be useful in the world'.

Alice would probably agree, but for her and her friends Guiding is about more than learning important skills – it is also a lot of fun.

In the late 1930s the Girl Guides Association worried that it was losing members to more commercial forms of leisure like the cinema, or the glamorous new dance halls. But despite the ascendancy of these rival attractions, Guiding remained popular among the young women of Bolton. Alice was one of nearly nine hundred local members and there were almost as many Brownies.

The Guides attended weekly meetings and rallies, marching with their company on special occasions and enjoying camping and hiking in the nearby Lancashire countryside. By the end of the year, the town's membership had won hundreds of proficiency badges between them, in such varied categories as Artist, Cobbler, Dancer and Pathfinder, as well as a host of craft-based skills such as Knitter, Embroideress and Needlewoman. Alice was already a gifted seamstress – many years later she will teach needlework at night school – and surely completed these latter tasks with ease.

In early May, both she and her best friend Elsie – who was excited to have just won her first badge – wrote about how the Guides were preparing for the upcoming coronation of George VI. Alice had a dress to alter, the one she would wear for the procession, and then the two girls spent the afternoon together at Hawthorne Street, reading, before heading off to their meeting. That evening they would practise walking behind the flag and sing 'Land of Hope and Glory' instead of the usual campfire songs.

They had talked incessantly about what the big day would be like and their own starring role in it. One lucky Bolton Guide – a girl older than Alice and Elsie – had been chosen to represent the town in London on Coronation Day itself. They were surely jealous when she reported back that she had had a 'fantastic' view from a spot on the Thames embankment and had seen the royal procession. Back in Bolton, Alice and Elsie were proud participants in the coronation morning parade, and saw the celebratory beacon lit up later in the day.

And the celebrations carried on – a month later they travelled to the County Coronation Rally in Manchester, which was attended by the leader of the Girl Guides herself, Lady Baden-Powell. They must have been thrilled to see her in real life. Bolton's Guides gave two keep-fit displays and four hundred of them staged a grand finale. Dressed in red, white and blue shirts, they formed themselves into an impressive human Union Jack.

It was a display of patriotism and loyalty that Lady

Baden-Powell would have been delighted with. When her husband and sister-in-law had established the Scouting and Guiding movements earlier in the century, supplementing other uniformed religious youth movements such as the Boys' and Girls' Brigades, their aim was to use such clubs to create good, orderly citizens who would use their leisure time productively, rather than spending it hanging around the streets.

But one did not preclude the other; the Pikes Lane girls were happy doing both.

A group of children stand in a ring on the grass, concentrating. One starts to chant, pointing to each of the others in turn: 'One, two, three, four, five, six, seven, all good children go to Heaven. Penny on the water, tuppence on the sea, thruppence on the railway, out goes she.' The moment a girl has been chosen the others squeal and scatter in every direction – the game begins.

When Senior II are asked to list their favourite games they each reel off several, naming nearly fifty between them. Most require little preparation, such as kick out ball (a more elaborate version of hide and seek) or hop flag (a form of hopscotch). Skipping is particularly popular and the girls know all the local rhymes off by heart. 'Mrs Mason broke a basin, on the way to Dobble station, how much did it cost her?' they chant as they jump.

Other activities take a little more organisation, such as the girls' favourite, rounders; although even this is played with whatever comes to hand, with an old piece of wood or a long piece of slate transformed into a makeshift bat. The girls take it very seriously and the game is extraordinarily popular among women in the town. There are around eighty work teams playing across two leagues and the best players achieve a measure of local celebrity. When asked to speak at the end of one important match, a local priest declares that he would far rather watch the town's women play rounders than sit through a men's cricket match at Old Trafford.

If not in their immediate streets and back lanes, the girls are often to be found in Queen's Park, the large Victorian park to the north of Pikes Lane School, with its pavilion, formal flower beds and lake, as well as tennis courts, open spaces for games and a playground. The girls mention the roundabouts frequently, although there are sometimes accidents. 'They'll break their bloody necks before long I'll bet, you know it's no bloody joke falling on stone flags and that's what will happen if they fall you know,' warns a park keeper.

Elsie spends the afternoon of Good Friday here with a group of friends (although not Alice; she's at Glazebury). 'We played rounders for a while and then passed on to the Pavilion,' Elsie remembers. 'I suggested playing French Cricket, which kept us busy for an hour. Afterwards we played at rolling down a hill. When we came to the pond we were told that a boy had killed a duck, which had sank to the bottom. On the way home we all agreed that we had enjoyed the outing.'

Sometimes the girls venture further afield and head into the surrounding fields. Three of them write about going fishing in the River Croal at Middlebrook, though it may not be a coincidence that those who do all have brothers. Mavis is one, claiming to have caught twelve fish on one trip out: 'It was much fun when a fish was biting because they gave a little tug.' Those who don't fish also appreciate the countryside. 'All the birds were singing as if they were glad summer had come,' writes one of the Joyces.

The girls are not always in each other's company and sometimes seem content to wander around on their own. One decides to make the best of a dull Good Friday by taking herself off to Queen's Park for a solo picnic of boiled ham sandwiches, hot cross buns and a bottle of milk. 'Afterwards I walked round till about half past three then I sat down on the grass and ate the rest of my buns and sandwiches,' she writes.

Another spends a frustrating Good Friday morning trying to clear the snow, 'but when I cleared it the snow came again so I left it to clear away itself because of there being snow showers'. Her afternoon was not much better: 'I didn't go anywhere special, only roaming the streets.' The day was redeemed by a trip to the cinema that evening to see Claudette Colbert in *She Married Her Boss*.

When the weather is too dreadful to allow outdoor play – or maybe just for a change – the girls have a range of indoor activities to keep them busy. Miss Kemp asks about their favourite choice here too and they offer up a range of options, such as knitting (Marion), sewing (Joyce D), embroidery (Annie), reading (Joan) and painting (Alice). 'Inside games are cards, snakes and ladders, dominoes, draughts, bob's your uncle and jigsaw puzzles, which I like very much,' one of her pupils tells her.

The way the girls spend their leisure time will change as they get older, of course. Already, many of these twelve-and thirteen-year-olds love to dance. Alice recently won a dance competition; Irene is a keen Morris dancer; and Jessie is following in the steps of her favourite film star, Shirley Temple, by learning how to do tap.

They are still too young to regularly frequent the town's many dance halls, although children are occasionally welcomed. When Walter Hood attends a trade union-sponsored dance at the Spinners' Hall he counts at least thirty, out of a crowd maybe three hundred strong. He enjoys watching four girls, aged about ten, perform 'a kind of ring-a-ring-a-roses' to the tune of a hornpipe, but sums up the atmosphere as 'that of a jolly party not a select dance'.

As they grow into their teens, dancing will become more important to the girls both as something to do with friends and also as a way of meeting boys, as the live music, dimmed lights and close contact between dance partners creates a sense of romantic possibility. Mass Observation estimates that there are more young people in attendance at Bolton's six main dance halls on a Saturday evening than there are in its many chapels and churches the following morning.

'Where can the young people meet unless they get to the places where they can dance? They can't get the best floors and bands in the Sunday Schools,' explained one dance hall manager. He added as an afterthought, 'We aren't to blame for what happens after.'

Bolton's dance halls were open from eight till eleven every evening except Sundays. Mass Observers visited, of course, and described their surroundings – 'a band on a dais, shaded lights, a polished floor' – but often paid closer attention to the dancers themselves. One made a sketch of different couples to show where a man most often positioned his hand on his partner's back. Another listed the colour of every single dress worn: 'The most popular colour amongst blondes was turquoise blue; the brunettes preferred a mixed colour floral pattern.'

They took the opportunity to dance, too, finding it 'hard work steering on a small floor among the crowd; couples constantly bump; no apologies, just grins'. Hood – who always had his Mass Observation hat on – tried to take the opportunity to elicit some extra opinions. 'How are you enjoying the dance?' he asked his partner. 'Alright. But I don't like talking when I'm dancing,' she rebuffed him. Hood wrote up the exchange later. 'So I put my best foot forward,' he said.

Many of the Observers, like Hood, were male and unmarried and he, for one, was quite taken with the female dancers. 'It hits me between the eyes when I go to the Palais,' he said, of the Palais de Danse with its oak and walnut sprung dance floor and capacity of six hundred. But it wasn't its size that struck him. It was 'the girls – how smart they look – how well they use colour; and then think of them coming out of the mill with the cotton waste in their hair'.

A self-confessed poor dancer, he was even more impressed with their level of skill: 'To me, the way they dance is far superior to that of Birmingham or London, and is streets ahead of undergraduates at Oxford. They're in another world.'

When we speak to the sons and daughters of the Pikes Lane girls, several of them will tell us that their parents met in the dance hall. Dancing, said a Mass Observer in

1937, had become 'an essential part of any youth's social equipment'. For those who struggled, numerous lessons took place 'in top floors and front rooms all over Bolton', while the bigger halls ran learners' nights.

Annie's future husband John isn't a dancer when they first meet. He has always claimed two left feet but begins to hate the fact that he can't show her off on the dance floor. Training with the Royal Navy in Plymouth during the war, he will book himself lessons so he can impress her when he returns to Bolton. They will carry on dancing all their married lives.

For the moment, though, the girls are happy with more childish pursuits, and it is carnival day in Bolton. Children put on fancy dress or wear the uniforms of their marching bands and dance groups, ready to take their places in a procession through the town. The organisers — Bolton Royal Infirmary — claim it's the best such event in the whole of the north of England.

The carnival committee hopes for dry weather — even though it's mid-August, last year's event had been a washout and takings were considerably down. Before the introduction of the NHS, money is desperately needed to help build new wards and address the hospital's three thousand-pound deficit. This doesn't stop one man describing those collecting money as 'a set of bloody scroungers'.

The procession starts to assemble after lunch, and children fidget as they wait. Leading it off are men from the Fire Brigade, a Charlie Chaplin 'capering about, twirling a stick', and a twelve-year-old girl carrying a Union flag. Many of those following are dressed as characters or celebrities — a

Mae West lookalike makes a particular impression on a group of pub-goers, as does Westhoughton's beauty queen. Bands of all descriptions, troupes of Morris Dancers, farmers and decorated cycles are all in the mix.

The procession snakes slowly towards the carnival grounds. Those watching are mostly women and girls, including some who are still in their cotton-covered mill clothes. A few hold their carnival programmes aloft, hopeful that they will receive a reward for doing so from the 'Mystery Woman' moving through the crowds.

Tom Binks – who combines Mass Observing with his mill job – is watching the procession. He makes extensive notes on the 162 different groups and individuals who pass but finds the occasion surprisingly flat: 'The crowd seemed to me on the whole very uncarnival-like. They were extremely dull and showed no animation.'

When a funeral cortège momentarily moves into the procession's path, it causes little comment, though some of the men remove their hats until the hearse and carriages have gone past. Binks wonders if the weather is affecting the mood: it is a dull afternoon with spotty showers, and it had rained steadily right up until the start of the procession.

The carnival itself boasts a fun fair and numerous side shows including coconut shies, skittles, palmistry and a 'ham slashing competition'. Though those keen to see Billy – 'the largest pig in the world' – will have to wait until the Christmas fair comes to town.

There are competitions galore, with total prize money of two hundred pounds and numerous cups and trophies to be won. Later, the judges will choose the best Morris dancers, fancy dress costumes, bands, dancers, tradesmen's displays, motor vehicles and the 'neatest, cleanest donkey'. The Challenge Rose Bowl is presented to the best-decorated street in Bolton. The carnival's baby show is the largest in Lancashire.

Children play an important role in the day's events. Several groups of teenage girls perform dances including tap, folk, a silk dance, a minuet and some swing. One audience member likes the swing dancing best: 'They're a lot better, more modern'; while another commends the enthusiasm of every group, commenting that 'Children take it far more serious than grown girls. They give their minds to it.'

The carnival's centrepiece is the crowning of the new Royal Infirmary Queen. It is an elaborate affair. The outgoing queen is dressed in silver; the queen-elect in lavender. There is a lot of bowing; presents and flowers are presented; words are said, and crowns are exchanged. The new queen moves through the crowds, and six young women, just a little older than the Pikes Lane girls, hold her train.

It is her job to present the prizes, but the timings are all out and everything is running late. She is looking a little tired now, and as she waits to perform her duties – 'trying to get out of the draught' – she nervously plays with the little finger of her left hand. A group of her friends a little distance away are trying to make her laugh, each pretending to wear a crown like hers, and she is not doing too well at hiding her giggles. When called upon to present the best brass band awards, she laughs again, self-consciously this time, and shakes hands rather awkwardly. A boy her own age comes to accept a prize, and they both blush.

As dusk falls, some of the prizes are yet to be awarded and

the meat raffle is yet to be drawn. At nine o'clock the jazz bands are still competing, though the refreshment tent has long since stopped serving and their presentation had been scheduled for 7.30. A decision is made to give the rest of the awards 'without any fuss'. A spectator approves: 'The sooner the bloody better, it's bloody cold now,' he mutters.

As the day comes to an end the hospital's organising committee hopes that another year of inclement weather has not damaged their fundraising efforts too badly.

8.

Sickness

The Royal Infirmary is not the only hospital in Bolton in need of financial support. Bolton's Isolation Hospital on Hulton Lane is run-down and understaffed, and the council has recently had to promise one hundred thousand pounds of investment. Infectious diseases such as measles and diphtheria are not always easy to control, though the town is grateful to have had no cases of smallpox since 1933. Scarlet fever is also on the wane.

Tom Harrisson, founder of Mass Observation, is keen to visit the Isolation Hospital, though he has to push to gain access. The local medical officer is reluctant to let him look round: it doesn't show his town's healthcare at its best.

A tall maid in uniform answers the bell and shows Harrisson into a small office with peeling lino. It is five days until Christmas and the matron is on the telephone, busy discussing preparations. They will have four trees this year, one more than last. She wants little dog decorations on the branches and no skimping on the coloured lights.

They go along the corridor, looking through the windows at the long, bare wards. One is full of children in red woolly coats. They spot the visitors and start pointing and calling to each other. It is an excitement, Harrisson thinks. There is little other diversion for them – certainly there are no toys to be seen. The matron tells Harrisson that she never employs local girls as nurses. They'd know the patients and start calling them by their Christian names. 'And you can't have it, you know.'

Next, they go out to the tuberculosis pavilion. It is a plain brick building, looking all the more miserable for the snow that has turned brown and slushy around it. Several patients can be seen through the windows, gaunt and thin in their beds. Some do recover, Harrisson is told. 'If they do it is wonderful,' he writes later. 'The will to live must indeed be a powerful thing in those poor bodies, for around them is no beauty or hope that may make life look worth living.' He is not alone in his condemnation. When another of the Mass Observation team visits, he offers a more succinct judgement: 'What a hellhole.'

Later in the year the tuberculosis patients will be moved out to free up beds, following the worst outbreak of diphtheria in the town since 1919. Two hundred people will be hospitalised, of whom twenty-three will not recover. Most of those who die are under ten; all are younger than twenty.

Mavis's older sister, Florence, has tuberculosis. She is a patient at Wilkinson's Sanatorium at Astley Bridge, the other place in Bolton where such patients are treated. Mavis visits on Easter Sunday and mentions it in her school essay the following week. 'We passed many fields and a lake,' she writes of the journey, presumably referring to the reservoir owned by Bolton waterworks, downhill from the sanatorium. It is only a couple of miles north of the town centre but feels a world away from the crowded streets near Pikes Lane. 'The place is situated in the midst of the country and one gets plenty of fresh air,' writes Mavis.

Mavis is one of the Hebron Hall girls, but her attendance is infrequent, and she is unsure about some aspects of religion when asked to address them in her essays. She writes of Heaven as an imaginary place, made up so that 'people who die can die happy'. She is similarly sceptical about Hell, which she dismisses as a threat 'to make the bad people good'.

When asked to write about Jesus she suggests that 'sometimes he was a little too religious', before deciding against this and crossing it out, offering platitudes instead about Jesus as 'a thoughtful man because he always thought about the poor and the sick and how to make them happy'. Nonetheless, Miss Kemp is impressed, telling Mass Observation that she is pleased to have 'one doubter'.

The number of people becoming ill or dying from tuberculosis was declining in the first half of the twentieth century. But there was still no known cure; that would have to wait until the discovery of streptomycin in 1947. It remained a feared disease, and the girls knew how deadly it could be. Joan was the most recent to have been bereaved – her mother had died of it a few months earlier, four days after Christmas 1936. Her grandmother, distraught herself at the loss of her daughter, had since been doing her best for Joan and her sister.

We don't know where Mavis's sister Florence became infected, or for how long she had been ill, but tuberculosis was most virulent in overcrowded surroundings and among an undernourished population. Her family – three girls and a boy, along with their parents – lived in a little terraced house in the dense streets to the south the school, surrounded by mills.

Poor air quality increased the risk, and a dense smoke hung over the town for much of the time, emanating from the tens of thousands of coal fires on which local people cooked and heated their homes. The factory chimneys further polluted the air, pumping out regular trails of black smoke. There were byelaws that attempted to control what left a factory chimney – grit, for example, was forbidden – but in 1937 there had been only fourteen prosecutions in the previous ten years. Fines were usually about twenty shillings, an inconsequential amount to the big firms, a Mass Observer was told.

Bolton will struggle with air pollution for another generation to come – things only really started to improve in the 1970s, when gas central heating became commonplace – and the repercussions followed the girls for the rest of their lives. Joyce D was in her early sixties when she died of lung cancer. Her daughter blames the industrial smoke that she breathed in all her life.

Molly was another who would be chesty all her life – 'like everyone was chesty of that generation', says her daughter, who herself remembers fog 'so bad you could taste it', and the need to put the car windscreen wipers on to clear it. Tuberculosis had taken its toll on that family too. Molly's uncle had died at Wilkinson's Sanatorium in 1942, leaving his widow Hilda to run the little shop they owned alone; Molly would often go across to help.

In 1937, Mavis's sister Florence was just eighteen and had started work in the cotton industry when she had left Pikes Lane four years earlier. The long hours in the hot, humid conditions of the mill, in rooms that were often poorly ventilated, were not conducive to stopping the spread of a contagious air-borne disease like tuberculosis. An additional danger lay in the practice of 'kissing the shuttle', whereby weavers loaded the thread to be ready for use by sucking it through the shuttle eye, breathing in dirt and chemicals at the same time, as well as any germs that a previous worker might have left behind.

A link between mill work and respiratory diseases had been known for more than a century. The Lancashire doctor Sir James Kay had first drawn attention in the 1830s to the number of cotton workers he treated for what he called 'spinners' phthisis'. 'There's many a one as works in a carding-room, that falls into a waste, coughing and spitting blood, because they're just poisoned by the fluff,' says Bessy Higgins in Elizabeth Gaskell's 1854 novel *North and South*, of the conditions that will kill her.

But there had been little government action, then or since. It was the 1920s before byssinosis, as it had come to be known, was widely recognised as an industrial disease caused by prolonged exposure to cotton dust, and it was 1941 before there was any kind of compensation scheme. Particularly vulnerable were workers in the cardroom, mostly women, which was one of the dustiest places in the mill. Dust extractors were compulsory in 1937 but they were often inadequate.

Stopping the spread of tuberculosis had attracted a little more official attention. Government funding for the construction of sanatoria had been provided since before the First World War and benefits had been extended to the wives and children of insured working men. Some local authorities had converted isolation hospitals previously used for smallpox cases into tuberculosis sanatoria; elsewhere local philanthropists had donated buildings.

This was the case in Bolton, where Thomas Wilkinson gifted his residence to the council. It opened as Wilkinson's Sanatorium in 1910. By 1937 it had been equipped with beds for fifty patients and the modern X-ray apparatus that was, by then, being used to diagnose the disease. It may have been where Florence first saw the faint mottling on the shadow of her lung, the earliest sign of pulmonary tuberculosis.

Frustratingly, Wilkinson's Sanatorium was one of the few Bolton hospitals that Mass Observers didn't visit – or at least no record survives if they did. Old photographs show the main building in the background with outdoor huts for use by patients; they were able to swing to face the sunlight. As well as isolating patients and attempting to prevent the spread of the disease to their families, sanatoria like this one offered a treatment regime based on fresh air, rest and a healthy diet. Patients were moved into the outside shelters as much as possible, and windows and verandas kept open.

'Very cold' was Mavis's description when she went to visit her sister.

The Isolation Hospital and Wilkinson's Sanatorium are two of several hospitals in Bolton that cater for different types of patient and offer different forms of medical care.

Townley's Hospital is for those who can afford nothing better. It has developed from the workhouse buildings adjoining and still has some of the shame of the workhouse attached. It is also in desperate need of investment. The hospital's X-ray machine, for example, is 'quite out of date', the radiologist tells Tom Harrisson.

It includes a block for patients with a mental illness, which further stigmatises it in the eyes of many in the town. When two Observers visit, one writes up his notes under the heading 'Personal Impressions of the Mental Block', before crossing out the title and replacing it with a new one: 'The Home of the Living Dead'. The building is oppressive and stuffy. It has plain brick walls, mouldering woodwork and bare floors.

'Poor buggers,' writes one of the Observers. 'I have been in low-down doss houses, but at least they're alive.' In one room they pass a man in a bed with no teeth and a glazed expression, who is mumbling something about wanting a gun. The Observers sympathise; they'd be taking a gun to themselves before long if they had to stay here, they think. 'Perhaps the poor old bugger wasn't so mad after all.' They leave feeling slightly sick, glad to get out.

In the years before a National Health Service, which wasn't to be introduced until 1948, patients had to pay in order to get a better quality of care, whether for mental or physical health. The Royal Infirmary was Bolton's 'voluntary' hospital, meaning it relied on charitable donations supplemented by patient contributions. Those in employment could pay twopence a week through their employer (or a penny if they were under twenty-one) and were required to bring a certificate with them, confirming that their contributions were up to date, before they could be treated. 'If you have no money you can't have a doctor,' writes one of the Pikes Lane girls. 'We pay for bandages, ointments and medicine which I don't like,' explains another.

When a Mass Observer visits the Royal Infirmary, his report is much more positive. The Infirmary is particularly proud of its expensive rubber flooring, which deadens nearly all sound. There are new twin operating theatres 'which are as modernly equipped as any in the country', and a sunlight room in which a little girl is sitting, 'clad in a raincoat and anti-glare spectacles'.

And yet patients still have to wait for treatment. Hearing problems affect many in the town, not least those who are exposed to the ferocious noise in the mills. There are four hundred people on the list to be assessed but the aural department is very small. The Observer is told that waiting times can be as long as twelve months.

As a voluntary hospital, the Royal Infirmary's running costs are also supplemented by fundraising. At a time of rapid advances in treatment and technology, the need for this is increasing. Organising events such as the summer carnival takes considerable time and energy, and there is only so much money to go round. The Observer has a simple solution: 'all hospitals should be nationalised'.

Overall, though, he concludes, 'The Bolton Infirmary is a very good hospital, and one wonders why Lancashire people still seem to prefer their herbalists and witch-doctors when they have all the facilities of modern medical science ready at their doorstep.'

There's a crowd of women around one of the open-air stalls at Bolton Market. A stoutish woman dressed as a nurse is keeping up a constant patter as she hands out samples of a yellow–brown liquid. It is early evening and many of the women are mill girls who have come straight from work.

The stallholder waits until she has the attention of those around her and then, with a theatrical flourish, produces a stethoscope and pulsometer. She attaches the pulsometer to her left hand and squints down at it for a few moments. 'Nothing wrong!' she announces. 'Good heart, good digestion, good liver, kidneys working.' She pauses to relish the effect on her audience and then beckons to one of the watching women. 'Let's take the little lady here.'

Her guest holds out her hand shyly and the stallholder attaches the pulsometer to her finger. 'Aha, you have a clenching pain here,' she tells her, pointing to the woman's groin. The stallholder continues with the whispered air of a fortune teller, though her practised voice carries to the rest of the crowd. 'Sometimes when you come down from a bus you feel as though you'd fall forward. When you bend down you feel as though you won't even get up again. Sometimes it leaves you for a week, a fortnight, but it comes back.'

She pauses, to leave space for contradiction, but the woman is looking down at the pulsometer, awed. 'URIC ACID!' The stall holder's voice is suddenly raised in a triumphant diagnosis. She removes the pulsometer and offers the woman a bottle: 'You need medicine.' The woman takes it, and hands over her money.

The Mass Observer watches as the stallholder rolls through different women and different ailments – anaemia, rheumatism, palpitations and more. There is only one man, who is seeking medicine for hair loss. Everyone acquiesces and takes the medicine offered. One former customer approaches the stall with the news that her relative is very much better. 'Ah well, that's the main thing,' comes the reply, as the saleswoman occupies herself with the mixing of more coloured liquids.

The market is busy and humming with noise. Women are here to meet each other, chat, look around. It has the atmosphere of a fairground, thinks the Mass Observer present. The traders are good at what they do, and the most entertaining are those selling herbs or cures. It is these 'who are the most fluent, cheerful, give the best show'.

On another stall, a man is selling mandrake root, with instructions on how to make mandrake wine. 'It's the only herb that will cure every illness of the human anatomy. Look at me,' he says. 'I've been told I have the best physique in this place. I'll strip with any man in the town.' He says he's fifty-five; the Observer thinks he looks a healthy forty. He keeps up a steady patter, never repeating himself, holding the full attention of the crowd. 'It contains the only five vitamins in the whole world that can purify your blood and bile. It's in the Bible,' he says, flourishing the holy book and smacking it hard.

The Observer gets talking to another proprietor of a stall, who has seen him taking notes and is wondering what he is doing:

'There was three of them in here this morning, writing. Going round the stalls measuring letters they was.'

'Oh really?' feigns the Observer.

'Yes, I thought you was one of them perhaps. Don't know what they was after.'

The Observer tells him that he's just here to see what

people are buying . . . for advertising purposes, he adds. The proprietor jumps into selling mode. He supplies the actresses of Bolton, he says, who always ask for Dubarry cream. They won't have any other kind. And has he tried this baby powder? It only costs sixpence. It's so much better than the talc powders made by the more well-known companies. He knows, because he has tried – it cured him of a face rash in no time. Though he supposes that all those powders are made of much the same thing; it's the smell you pay for. This one has special antiseptic things in it . . . it says on the tin. Look! he says, holding it out towards the Observer.

The market sells all sorts of other goods as well, of course. In June, Mavis is there with her mum to get some cakes and fruit to take to her sister in advance of another visit to see her at Wilkinson's. Mavis gets a treat too and is allowed to choose some comics at the bookstall. She doesn't say whether or not they pause to glance at the alternative medicines, though of course they are desperate for a cure.

Florence won't stay in the sanatorium. Treatment there is supposed to last for as long as a patient needs it, but there is a waiting list for beds and, like many sanatoria across the country, patients have to be discharged to make room for others. We don't know when Florence leaves, but she is back home by the following spring, with her family anxiously watching over her decline, her coughing seeming to fill the small house.

Mavis and her mother continue to try and tempt her with special food and treats but Florence still loses weight, another symptom of the disease even when patients continue to eat. Ninety-two Bolton patients will have died of the disease by the end of 1937, one-third of whom are in their twenties and early thirties. Florence dies on 1 March 1938, aged just nineteen. Her death certificate lists marasmus – severe malnutrition – as the chief cause of death, followed by tuberculosis of the larynx and lungs.

9.

Holidays

Wakes Week is around the corner and a holiday feeling is in the air. For ages now everyone has been swapping suggestions on where to go and the newspapers have been full of adverts for places to stay. Mass Observation estimate that around half of Bolton's population will manage to leave town for the week. Most of the rest will get away for at least part of it or for day trips.

Wakes Week is the period during which the town's mills shut down. It is a Lancashire tradition that predates the industrial revolution, when the time was needed by factory managements for annual maintenance. Dates are staggered across the different towns; the Bolton holiday begins on the last Saturday in June, and the town 'almost literally closes down'.

Those who will be away for the full seven days ask neighbours to keep an eye on their house, promising to bring back a stick or two of rock in return. Women's hairdressers are fully booked – most customers want perms – and public baths are crowded. An employee at a dry-cleaners reports that they are ten times busier than normal; a policeman even has to be employed to control the queue. A grislier upturn in business is reported by the Destitute Animals Centre, who will put down more cats and dogs this week than any other.

In the centre of town on Saturday evening, the last shopping Saturday before the holiday, a Mass Observer stands and watches a clogged, shawled old woman with yellowed white hair, who stands in the gutter and drunkenly sings 'God Save the King'. The crowds ignore her, intent on their purchases. In the stores, items are disappearing off the shelves: suitcases, underwear, dresses, toothbrushes, toothpaste, combs, ribbons, cosmetics. Shop windows are full of displays of swimsuits and beach toys, and large signs promise holiday bargains. One shop, which sells waterproofs and umbrellas, caters to the more pessimistic holidaymaker, promising 'holiday rainwear'.

One housewife has already bought several holiday frocks from Woolworths. Once she might have worried that others would be wearing the same dress, but these days she doesn't fret over it – it's just the way it is now there's mass production, and 'after all,' she says, 'men are always dressed in the same damn way'.

Others are saving some purchases for when they arrive, so they can save room in suitcases: 'You get Woolworths and Littlewoods there so it's just the same.' Canvas shoes are often left as a holiday purchase; last summer a shoe shop in Blackpool sold five thousand pairs over one weekend for 2s 11½d a go, causing a local shortage of halfpennies.

But if shoes can wait until they get there, food often

can't. Many families take the bulk of their week's shopping with them, to be cooked by the landladies they stay with. Costs can be cut by placing a large order with the Co-op beforehand or saving up tinned goods for months in advance. Groceries are cheaper at home than on holiday and children are less likely to fuss, mothers think, if they can eat the food they are used to.

At 5.30 on the Friday evening, the red light at the mills signals the start of the holiday. One of the Mass Observers heads to the bus station to see those quickest to get away. On the way he overhears two corporation workmen grumbling to each another. 'I asked the bloody gaffer to let me off at half past four, but he wouldn't, the bugger.'

The bus station is already busy – the first ride to Blackpool leaves in less than an hour – and the conductors are looking harassed. One driver is remonstrating with an elderly lady who is refusing to part with her luggage and put it in the storage compartment. She is adamant: 'Do you think I was born yesterday, lad?'

The following morning the exodus continues. Another Mass Observer joins a train excursion to New Brighton. In the carriage two men are deep in the *Sunday Referee* and a couple sit holding hands and saying nothing. He compiles a list of some of the things he sees, with the apparent randomness typical of Mass Observation: nineteen children, twenty-nine men without hats, four bowlers, fourteen caps, forty-two trilbies, seven girls without stockings, two buckets and spades.

In 1937, most workers were not yet entitled to paid holidays. The culmination of two decades of campaigning was to come the following year, when the Holidays with Pay Act (1938) endorsed the principle of an annual period of paid leisure time to all full-time workers. When the act was passed, fifteen and a half million full-time workers had no right to a paid holiday.

In order to afford to go away, many workers started saving as soon as the previous year's holiday ended. The Co-op scheme was one of the most popular, with as many members as there were homes in Bolton. Churches, factories and pubs often had saving clubs of some sort too.

Those who spent the week in Bolton also needed to save up in advance if they could, for there would be no wages while the factories were closed; the last Friday in June was the last payday for a while. Informal arrangements with shopkeepers might help – from the spring, many traders would start allowing customers to add a few pence more onto their bills towards food for the holiday period. Without this, the poorest, who would be staying at home, would struggle to get enough to eat.

In the autumn of 1937 Mass Observation ran another of their competitions in the town, advertised in the *Bolton Evening News* and asking people to send in an account of 'How I want to spend my holiday'. Some of the replies were happy accounts of holidays spent that year or anticipations of ones to come. But many came from those who could only dream about a holiday away. 'How I *should have liked* to spend my holidays' would be a better title, commented one old man. He lived a little to the south of Pikes Lane in Venice Street, a name that belied the setting, and concluded that 'I shall have to go on sending for guide books and leaving the rest to my imagination.'

One respondent even wondered if the competition was a joke – the prize money of five pounds and five shillings seemed fantastical to him. He was unemployed and dependent on the Public Assistance Committee that administered the dole; his daughter was in the infants' department at Pikes Lane.

'Well, here goes, joke or not, I'll bite,' he wrote, 'and let you know how one on the PAC would spend a good holiday with pay, providing the PAC did not hear of it, and knock the good out of it by telling him how long five pounds and five shillings should last him at home . . . but I will forget that I am one of them for the time being and imagine I am all packed and all set for a good holiday with pay.'

He imagined going to Douglas on the Isle of Man and enjoying 'rest, change, exercise and pleasure'.

Twelve-year-old Joyce D has never been away for a holiday. In 1937 her parents have four children to feed, with more to come. She is the eldest; her youngest sister is still a baby. Her father, John, is a miner by trade. He started down the pit when he was the same age that Joyce is now, but in adulthood it suits him. He is a small, fierce man, and at just five foot tall he has a miner's build.

But the 1930s is not a good decade for the coal industry. John has to pick up what work he can, and he struggles to hold down a job. When his son Thomas dies of pneumonia in 1930, aged four, the death certificate records John as a stoker at the brickworks. The death of her little brother is probably one of Joyce's earliest memories; she is certainly old enough to remember when a second tragedy hits the family in 1933, when baby Doris dies. By the time Cawson makes his pen sketches of the Pikes Lane girls in 1937, John is scraping by as a carter.

The 1939 register simply notes that he is an unemployed collier, although at least by then Joyce has left school. She becomes the family's only earner when she enters the mill. No wonder that her parents hadn't felt able to encourage her scholarship ambitions.

We don't know how John felt about his struggle to provide for his family and the lack of paid leisure. But we have a possible answer in the entry submitted to Mass Observation's holiday competition by another miner. This man was a year John's senior, living in the nearby town of Westhoughton with his wife and three children. He, too, had lost a small son. This is what he wrote:

> I am a collier. I work hard in dust and dark. I
> would like to spend my holidays in some quiet
> seaside place far from the pit. I want to take my
> wife and kiddies with me and give them the rest
> and healthy air and experience they deserve. I
> am a man that wants to have health and strength
> to carry on my work for years to come. I want
> to ramble along the sea shore and lie in the sun
> which for eight hours a day I never see. I want
> to have a drink when I need one or a visit to the
> pictures. I am a man that likes a little fishing and
> that would also be nice on holiday. But alas I
> shall be very lucky indeed if I get all these things.
> We don't always get what we want, but why
> grumble there are better times ahead. So cheerio.

Joyce's mother may also have recognised the answer given by a female competition entrant:

> Instead of preparing meals for my family, it would be a real holiday for me to be waited on. I would love to stay at a hotel and have everything done for me. For ten years things have not been too prosperous, money has been scarce, and holidays have been make-believe. It would be a joy going in to breakfast, washed and dressed in nice clothes, then rising from the table knowing that someone else would clear and wash-up. I am tired. I just want a rest from everything one does and everything one sees for the rest of the year.

Joyce spends most of the week in Bolton, though it's a very different Bolton to usual: there is no clatter of clogs, no smoke. Most of the shops are shut and cinemas complain of their lowest takings in the year. Mass Observer Charles Madge thought that Bolton looked its best in holiday week – 'for the first time beautiful in its own right'.

There is, of course, the annual fair, though Mass Observation is dismissive of the clientele: 'the usual strolling girls, many of them in slacks, and groups of youths. They seemed to be mainly of the poorer paid workers, and of what would have been called in Victorian days the "improvident" type.' By evening there are the usual groups round the pubs and more inebriation than normal perhaps. 'One man, so drunk that he couldn't see, staggered along eating a currant bun with his eyes closed.'

Joyce also takes the chance to get out of the town. A

twopenny tram ride can take her into the fields, and though she can still see the factory chimneys, at least they're not smoking and she can be surrounded by birds and flowers. She loves it. When, a couple of months earlier, Miss Kemp had asked what she wanted to be when she grew up, she had suggested a shop assistant because then she would have Wednesday afternoons off and could 'go for lovely walks in the country'.

Earlier in the year she'd described going out into the countryside with her grandma and noticing 'the tiny heads of daffodils just peeping above the grass. We went to see the reservoir which was nearly overflowing and when the sun shone on the water it looked like silver.' When Cawson made his hasty pen sketch of Joyce he described her as a child with a 'very poor vocabulary'. Her essays suggest a flair for language; maybe he was too quick to dismiss this small, poorly dressed little girl.

Joyce probably went out to local beauty spot Barrow Bridge. Mass Observers didn't think much of it: 'a half-acre muddy boating lake at the edge of the paddling pool, which is generally out of use, the archery range, the tea-house and the slot machines. At the bottom of the lane there are cane-sellers, sweet and ice-cream stalls, though you can spend a pleasant afternoon there without spending any money.' They did at least admit that the surrounding countryside was beautiful, accessed via 'the sixty-three steps' that had once enabled workers to get to and from the mill – now demolished – at the top.

The girls didn't write any essays about their June holidays, but several of them mentioned Barrow Bridge when they wrote about what they'd done over the long

Easter weekend earlier that year. Joyce had gone on Easter Saturday, with Irene and some other friends. 'There were not many people there when we arrived, but later on the people came like a swarm of bees,' she wrote. They took their tea with them to eat outside, went on the rowing boats and climbed the sixty-three steps into the hills (their shoes got stuck in the mud, Irene reported), before buying sweets for the journey home.

But even Joyce's family managed to get out of Bolton once during Wakes Week, and the highlight was a trip to the seaside town of Southport. We don't know exactly when they went, but it's likely they joined one of the outings that ran every day that week.

Mass Observer Joe Wilcock does the trip on the Thursday. It's a good one for the kids, the porter tells him – it's cheap and they don't get back so late, not like trips to Blackpool, which arrive back at midnight. Certainly there seem to be a lot of children at the station, and as the train starts to fill he is amused by the family patterns: first the father a yard or so ahead, looking through the windows to find room; then children straggling after with their buckets and spades; finally, finding a compartment, they disappear inside, their mother going in last with a look of visible relief.

Wilcock notices that the quality of dress seems poorer than on other trips he has made; two of the women in his carriage he spots immediately as millworkers – the oily dirt under their nails and the tiny flecks of cotton on their hats give them away. He will later be struck by the contrast between the poor day-trippers, who go to window-shop, and the well-dressed clientele in the more expensive stores. Southport is a popular shopping destination for the middle classes, so the contrast is more obvious here than in somewhere like Blackpool.

On the sands the trippers congregate in family groups. Nearly all of them carry paper bags from which they take neat sandwiches of salmon, ham or jam, and apples or oranges. Some have also brought flasks of tea. Those who haven't get their drinks from a nearby stall – sixpence for a jug of hot water; eightpence for tea with milk and sugar. 'It's alright if you've got plenty of money,' a woman tells Wilcock. 'They know you're coming in the cafes when you go in, it costs you enough for a pot of tea!' Her husband agrees and nods sagely. 'It's alright for a young single chap on his own, he can afford his steak and chips. Wait now till you get wed and then you'll not find it so easy.'

Wilcock wanders into the funfair but it's quiet. A chained monkey pulling a bell draws his attention to the 'jungle caves'. 'See the world', the board announces, and the men who take his money are in sailors' uniform. He sits in a small boat and floats past several tableaux portraying different countries.

The cheaper amusements are more popular, and in the park the bathing pool is busy with children playing in the water or enjoying the small paddle boats. Wilcock stops to chat to a young lorry driver from Bolton, who is in Southport for the week but who is bemoaning his misfortune: 'There's nowt but old women here. I came here because I knew a girl who was coming, but she buggered off with another bloke.' He is now consoling himself with races with his mate around the miniature car track.

In the early evening a band strikes up in an enclosure in

the park. They haven't sold more than half their tickets, maybe because the music carries and the day-trippers are congregating on the street benches outside to listen for free. When dusk falls, dozens of tiny lamps are lit in the branches of trees and crevices of buildings all along the main street. Families walk up to see them and a mother whispers to her little girl that this is what fairyland looks like.

The crowds on the train home don't seem as tipsy as they do returning from the Blackpool trips, Wilcock thinks, nor is there singing or even much conversation. Most people are quiet and look tired. Several children lean against parents and fall asleep. They get into Bolton just after eleven o'clock, and those with little ones have to nearly drag them up the station steps to home.

Joyce doesn't have long to wait until all of her playmates are back again. The holidaymakers have been unlucky with the weather this year, and by midweek people are starting to head home. The first to return are mainly families, who haven't enough dry clothes for the children. Others stick it out and, when they return on Saturday, the first properly hot day of the week, there's an ice-cream seller at the train station to meet them. It's such a shame, he says, when they've been away all week, to get this weather only when they come home. But at least it means he's doing a brisk trade.

Others of the Pikes Lane girls had been on day trips like Joyce. Elsie and Irene had both been to Southport too, but there were many other potential destinations. A thirty-two-page booklet produced by the railway company detailed the extra trains put on especially for holiday week, to destinations across the north west, North Wales and even further afield, with trips to London and Edinburgh. 'Have you decided on your holidays this year? Why not Great Yarmouth and Gorleston-on-Sea? The Playground for Workers and a Paradise for Children', ran the tagline on one pamphlet.

Some of the luckiest girls went away for longer. Some went to visit family: Marion went to her aunt in Ormskirk; Alice, as usual, to hers in Glazebury. One girl had been to the Isle of Man, one of the more expensive holiday options and a trip that her friends were jealous of, with its feeling of going overseas.

But the most popular destination for the Pikes Lane children was, of course, Blackpool, and virtually all of the girls had been there one time or another, whether for day trips or longer.

In Wakes Week Mass Observer Walter Hood takes a day trip to Blackpool, and on the train he watches two girls, both in blue, while away the journey, which lasts slightly more than an hour. He thinks they are in their mid-teens, so they're probably too old to be any of our Pikes Lane girls, but then he has no children himself, and the age of young teenage girls can be difficult to guess.

Most of the carriage is quiet, but the girls start pointing things out from the window. One pesters her dad to look up as they pass Chorley Ammunition works ('See dad, there's the new works!') and sometimes several people turn their heads ('There's a swan!'). The girls make noises to the rhythm of the wheels, and when they're bored of doing that, they sing a song: 'Let's all sing like the birdies sing. Tweet tweet tweet tweet tweet.'

Then they quieten down and begin talking to each other too softly for Hood to hear. They show each other the different things they have brought with them. Heads together, they pore over some kind of medallion – he can't really see it very well – and they are laughing.

When their bags' contents have been thoroughly sifted there is a silence for a moment. Then:

'Can you throw your voice?'

'Eh? What do you mean?'

'You know, like a ventra– ventra–' she laughs, 'you know what I mean.'

'A ventre-ologuist you mean. Alright, what shall we do?'

'Oh! Say something. Like "Hello".'

The 'hellos' echo round the carriage. The woman with them – presumably a mother – laughs but also chastises: come on now, that's enough.

'Hello, hello,' they continue, quieter, and trying to say it without moving their lips.

Ventriloquism exhausted, they wander into the corridor. When they come back there is only one question: 'Are we nearly there?'

They are, and as the train stops the girls are the first to be ready and onto Blackpool's platform. 'Come on!' they yell.

10.

Blackpool

It is Sunday 5 September 1937 and Miss Kemp is in Blackpool. She'd been looking forward to the long weekend in the holiday town, but it has been spoilt somewhat by the fact that she has been up all night with an upset stomach.

She is here with Miss Taylor, another teacher, who works at a junior school in Westhoughton, Bolton's smaller neighbour. We don't know how the two women got to know each other. They are a couple of years apart in age and perhaps they met at teaching college, or maybe it was their shared interest in Mass Observation that first brought them together.

Like Miss Kemp, Miss Taylor has been busy collecting schoolwork written by her pupils, though this weekend they are acting as Observers themselves, writing careful reports of what they see and do. Miss Kemp is feeling too rough to get much done but Miss Taylor has been carrying out her duties assiduously.

Yesterday she joined the long queue for the train station toilets twice, to give herself more time to collect overheard comments from those in the line: 'Oh hell! We've only five minutes to catch that train. Come on, love, you'll have to hold it.' And on Friday she had hung around outside the exhibition of the five-legged cow for so long that its attendants had started to make comments – but she was there to observe its visitors, not the cow. When a group finally arrived, she paid her twopence to follow them in and wrote down their reactions. 'Oh, that's genuine enough,' she heard a man say to a woman, 'but that' – and he pointed to a sign advertising a headless girl exhibition – 'is definitely a twist.'

This weekend Mass Observers have fanned out across the town and are sampling different types of holiday lodgings to suit a range of budgets and tastes. Tom Harrisson, in charge of the budget, has allocated himself the Norbreck Hydro – in later years to be renamed the Norbreck Castle Hotel – an imposing cream-façaded building on the seafront. Such places, charging a minimum of fifteen shillings a day, are 'where the Big Knobs hang out' and there are no guests from Bolton here.

While Harrisson enjoys the Norbreck's swimming pool, ballroom and solarium, other Observers are trying different boarding houses, charging less than half as much. The two local teachers have drawn the short straw and are sampling a typical 'kippax', the name for the unlicensed lodgings rented out informally by Blackpoolers and, at six shillings or less, the cheapest type of accommodation to be found.

The women are sharing a small eight-by-nine room in a terraced house in Cambridge Street, a fifteen-minute walk from the seafront. Their landlady will be sixty that month and she has never married. Without the steady flow of holidaymakers she would be poorly off indeed, although the regular turnover of guests is hard work. She always has mixed feelings when the holiday season comes to an end, although this won't be for another few weeks yet – no sooner have the throngs of summer visitors begun to dry up then the crowds start arriving for the famous illuminations.

But for the Lancashire women who stay here over the summer, a landlady's services are a welcome respite from the usual burden of responsibility for the household. Miss Taylor chats with a woman down at the beach, who tells her that she is looking forward to her dinner. 'Of course it makes a difference when you haven't to bother about cooking it.'

In return, guests have to give up a degree of independence, and the insistence of landladies on punctual mealtimes is one of the grumbles most frequently overheard by Mass Observers, who comment that 'these times, arbitrarily fixed and generally enforced by the landladies, control all the movements of people on sands and prom, as effectively and more exactly than the tide or weather'. Some of the Observers – though not Kemp or Taylor – notice charity boxes in their boarding houses, explained away by slightly embarrassed landladies, who say that 'visitors only pay into them as fines, when a) they are late for breakfast and b) when they spill food on the tablecloth'.

For younger guests there are further restrictions. Three girls of sixteen tell an Observer that they're planning to change lodging houses next year; they dislike their current landlady who has 'had it out with them' for talking from their bedroom window to boys in the house opposite. Even the smallest children might feel the weight of different expectations. When Miss Taylor asks her eight-year-old pupils to write about their holiday after their return to school, one tells her that 'When I was having my dinner I had to use a knife and fork.'

Back in Cambridge Street, Miss Taylor makes a careful inventory of the room: fawn, pink and green lino; chamber pot under the bed; a calendar illustrated with a picture of 'two jovial monks sampling the wine'. An empty bottle of soda water sits on the dresser, testament to her companion's attempts to settle her stomach during the night. She leaves Miss Kemp to sleep and goes down to breakfast on her own – overlooked in the dining room by a white-framed sculpture of Cupid – and then out into town.

Tom Harrisson knew that Blackpool was special. He reckoned that 95 per cent of Bolton's population had visited the nearby town on the coast of the Irish Sea, and so an investigation of holidaymaking there seemed an obvious focus of research.

At first, Mass Observers took day trips or weekend stays, but by August 1937 they had hired lodgings in the holiday town to act as their headquarters, and soon there was a steady stream of researchers going back and forth. Five investigators spent a full six months there, assisted by the usual coterie of interested local residents and Bolton-based Observers who made shorter trips.

Trips to Blackpool felt like a holiday of sorts for the Observers, too, and many of the southern, middle-class men and women who made up the team were both repelled by and drawn to the tackiness, the commercialism and the surrender to pleasure. Harrisson believed himself immune to the more mystical of Blackpool's attractions, comparing his own rationality to what he saw as the gullibility of working-class holiday makers. One day he set out to survey the myriad palm readers and fortune-telling machines, collecting forty-three different readings. He reported back triumphantly that he could now enjoy a lucky day every day of the week and every date of the month.

But the magic of Blackpool got to Harrisson eventually. 'The racket, the crowd, the heat, is tremendous,' he wrote. 'There is nothing else quite like it. Everything is infected by the spirit of mass enjoyment. Even the food. Whole stalls seem to be sprouting great pink and white spiders of sugared ice-cream, like the form of some heavenly sea, ready to blow into the mouth of anyone who breathes inwards; and this confectionery, like everything else in Blackpool, is special, Blackpoolish, and with a wonderful name – fairy floss.'

Blackpool's reputation went beyond the north west. From the second half of the nineteenth century, with the growth of opportunities for mass leisure, Blackpool had remained preeminent among the growing number of commercialised seaside resorts. The construction of two piers in the 1860s, another in the 1890s, and the opening of the Blackpool Tower by the end of the century cemented its position as a 'Wonderland of the World'.

In the interwar period it continued to grow, developing its parks, shops and amenities, while better transport links catered for ever-growing visitor numbers. By the mid-1930s, the town was hosting millions of holidaymakers a

year. The country's second underground car park was built
there in 1933 (the first was in Hastings) and the first multi-
storey car park in 1939.

The novelist and playwright J. B. Priestley drove to
the town in 1933, while on his trip around England. As
he got closer, he recalled, 'all the roads suddenly become
very straight and wide and display large cheerfully vulgar
advertisements. That is because they, like you, are going to
Blackpool. Even if you did not intend to go to Blackpool,
once you had got beyond Preston you would have to go
there. These roads would suck you into Blackpool. That is
what they are there for. There is no escape.'

It was a 'huge mad place', was Priestley's verdict, a
town against which 'places like Brighton and Margate
and Yarmouth are merely playing at being popular seaside
resorts. Blackpool has them all licked.' He added, 'I know
people who would have to go into a nursing home after
three hours of it.'

The beach is packed. A team of Mass Observers – 'one
with a Cambridge first in mathematics!' – have made a
careful count and calculated that there are ten thousand
people on the seven-mile expanse of sands. Many of them
are concentrated on the shorter stretch of beach and prom
between the north and south piers, where the tunes of
buskers overlap and stalls selling rock, oysters, postcards or
trinkets are doing a roaring trade. One of her pupils will
later give Miss Taylor an account of his holiday spending:
sixpence on a beach ball, sixpence on a kite, threepence on
string, twopence on a wafer and a final twopence on chips.

New for 1937 is a stall selling huge lollipops six inches

across, on a foot-long stick: 'Ten thousand licks, count 'em', reads the sign. The ice-cream carts are having to be replenished every couple of hours. Overhead, an aeroplane is flying back and forth trailing a huge pennant: 'COLD OVALTINE IS DELICIOUS'.

Mothers are snoozing in deckchairs or flicking through the newspaper while their children build sandcastles beside them. A number of fathers are down on the sand too, helping to build a castle or, in a few cases, making it themselves while the children 'dig aimlessly around'. Some of them – parents as well as children – will take a handful of sand back with them to Bolton, carefully carried in paper bags.

The sea is busy with children paddling and throwing beach balls. One of Alice's neighbours from Hawthorne Street was here earlier in the summer. She is also a senior pupil at Pikes Lane, although in a different class to Alice. As an only child, and with her father an overseer at the mill, her family can afford to spend a few days in Blackpool. She enters an account of her trip to Mass Observation's holiday essay competition, telling of how she played cricket on the sands almost every day, though the sea is also an attraction: 'After a running about playing at beach ball, into the sea I will go with my life-belt, and practice swimming. When I come out I will give myself a good rubbing and change, and I will feel ready for anything.'

Two small boys are pestering their parents for a donkey ride. 'Oh, let them go – they've mithered all week to go on,' says their mother. Their auntie decides to join them and, as soon as she's on, her sister grins and shouts to the donkey-handler, 'Give her donkey a reet good crack.' He does, but the donkey doesn't respond: 'The bugger won't run.' Elsewhere, Punch violently attacks Judy to shrieks of laughter from his young audience. A group crowd around an automatic weighing machine and a woman in her mid-fifties steps off: 'Eeeh, I were only eleven eleven last year,' she says, frowning.

When the tightrope walkers start performing on Central Pier, crowds gather underneath, squinting upwards and applauding. Camilla and Ernest are the two top stars: Camilla is handsome, wearing white naval clothes with a black bow tie and sailor's cap. Ernest is only twelve and has had to be granted special permission to perform by the Ministry of Labour. His favourite trick is to pretend to stumble, crying out, before saving himself at the last minute. Some of his audience can't watch, despite the large safety net. The small black shape of his body and long balancing pole can be seen from both of the other piers, silhouetted against the sea.

The local Blackpool children mostly disparage the crowds when they are asked their opinions of the town in the summer. 'You can't have a good swim without bumping into someone,' writes one; the visitors 'walk and talk as if they owned the place', reports another. Littering is a common grudge: the children say that during the holiday period the roads look 'like rubbish dumps', and the town is filled with people who 'throw their banana skins all over the place'. One declares that 'rude little children hit you with large iron spades', perhaps with the bruises – and maybe also the bruised pride – to show from the encounter.

A handful soften in a moment of generosity, having been told of the smoky towns from which the visitors come: 'We must not be selfish'; 'they deserve a nice holiday', they write. 'People arrive very happy but leave very sad,' observes another child.

One of the nine-year-olds writes a description of the holidaymakers that would have been worthy of any of the adult Mass Observers:

> In summer trains run all day long, people rush to open the compartment doors. Then they all run into shops which are crowded with visitors and friends. I then see them rushing away some in taxis and buses, some even walking, children asking to go on the sands and weeping because they could not. Other children were carrying cases for their mothers and fathers and tramping along for their lunch. After they all set off for the sands some was swimming all over the water, some making sandcastles and jumping over them and laughing when they fall, and then running in their bathing suits into the sea. Splashing, jumping, splash splash splash all romping and running all over the sands. It rained on them and some went crying.

Later, Miss Taylor goes to Louis Tussaud's waxworks, where she follows three children around the exhibitions. They recognise Gandhi and pause briefly in front of him: 'Look, that's Gandhi'; 'He's against Britain's rule.' Then the eldest child points out Nelson to her little sister, and, affectionately, 'Oh look – Baden-Powell'. They pass by the likenesses of politicians and statesmen without much comment and walk quickly past the 'ecclesiastical figures and big shots'.

They spend most time in front of the coronation tableau, although they also point out Gracie Fields to each other before leaving and wonder who that 'English film star' might be (it's Marlene Dietrich).

When they leave, Miss Taylor follows some adults around for a while, including a woman who stops opposite Alexander I of Yugoslavia and wonders 'is this Hitler?' Then she takes the tram to the Pleasure Beach.

She hasn't been there long when there's a shout of 'Miss Taylor', and two children rush up to her – a brother and a sister, from her school. They are on their own – their parents have gone to watch the football, and their grandma is down at the beach. 'I don't like sitting in a deck chair or riding about, I would sooner be seeing something,' the older girl writes about her holiday when she gets home. Her brother has just won a brooch on the penny slot machines.

They have strict instructions to return to their grandma by 4.30, they tell their teacher. They ask a passer-by what time it is. It's 4.30. They dash off.

Reginald Dixon, organist for forty years at the famous Tower Ballroom, claimed there was nowhere like Blackpool. 'And it wouldn't matter if they built a Tower at lots of places,' he told a Mass Observer. 'This one (he cocks his head skywards and westwards) – is that the right direction? – it would still be different. You see, it's sentiment. People come here, and then they get married, and their children come with them, and grow up with it, and get used to it.'

We don't know if Joyce D ever got to Blackpool when she was small, or if her parents continued to favour Southport. Either way, it certainly seems unlikely that her family's circumstances would have allowed them anything more than a day trip. She would never mention going on a childhood holiday to her own children.

As an adult her life remains hard: after starting in the mill at fourteen, she is transferred into munitions during the war and ends up as a spot welder for a car factory in Bolton. Her husband walks out on her when she's pregnant with her second child, never to be heard from by his children again, and her mother dies soon after. She moves back into her father's house and takes on an extra cleaning job, starting a shift at five in the morning so she can complete it in time to put in the hours at the factory. Her daughter wears a latchkey around her neck and learns how to start making the dinner before her mum gets home. Joyce will rarely be able to afford to go out, despite her many friends; she might treat herself to the occasional bottle of stout.

But some things, at least, are easier. Blackpool had been one of several seaside towns visited by Labour MPs in the summer of 1937 as part of the 'seaside campaign' to rally support for the call for holidays with pay. Some of the Pikes Lane girls might have paused to listen, though they may not have recognised the speakers. The Holidays with Pay Act was passed the following year – encouraging and supporting employers to provide paid holidays rather than making them compulsory – but the principle had become near universal by 1945.

The extension of paid holidays coupled with rising wages means that a few days in the seaside resort is no longer beyond the reach even of poorer families. It means that Joyce can take her own children to Blackpool when Wakes Week comes around, sometimes joined by a sister or a cousin.

They will stay full board, and even half a century later her daughter will still remember the strictness of the mealtimes. They will go on the coach, rather than the train, because it costs less, but when they're there Joyce will give her children a shilling a day to spend, and they will wander through the town. Sometimes they'll spend the whole day at the Tower Ballroom and Joyce will get up to dance with one of her sisters. It will be something she saves for all year long, and every June she will sew a pocket into her corset to keep her money safe while she's there.

11.

Coronation Day

Constance steps out of her front door and grins. Lockbank Street, where she lives at number 17, is a small, cramped row of twenty houses, darkened by the soot of the three mills that overshadow it. But today it is a mass of colour, criss-crossed with bunting and streamers in red, white and blue. Today, George VI will be crowned.

It is May 1937, and the whole town is dressed up for the occasion. Lockbank Street has made a special effort, eyeing the prize for Bolton's best-decorated street. Edith Wigley, a young woman living a couple of doors down from Constance, at number 11, has co-ordinated the entry. She lost her newborn son last Christmas and, despite the grief – or maybe to distract from it – she has thrown herself into the coronation preparations, cajoling each household to do its bit.

To do well in the competition, every house has to participate or marks will be lost, say the judges, who stress that 'colour schemes, regularity of streamers and every house pulling its weight' will inform their decision. They warn that they will be paying attention even to the symmetry of the street's curtains.

Edith's work pays off, and the judges praise Lockbank Street as 'the most uniformly decorated of all'. It is one of two winners of the first prize of two pounds, which will later be spent on the street party.

She will tell her children about this, Constance thinks – and, in time, she does.

Bolton is enjoying coronation fever. Forty-five thousand tulips have been specially planted in the town's parks. Mill workers are to be given the day off. Bolton Savings Bank is promising a free gift of ten shillings to all children born within a few days of the coronation; nine mothers will eventually benefit. The Pikes Lane girls are most excited by the arrival of hairdresser Jean Black ('of London and Paris') bringing some metropolitan glamour with a 'demonstration of coronation hair styles' at the Empress Hall.

At school there is a lot of chatter about the coronation. Constance is proud of Lockbank Street, and other girls have news too. Dora's street won a consolation prize for 'triumphing most gallantly over its difficulties'. Its residents had their effort sabotaged by heavy winds that blew all their decorations away. Once they had been patiently put up again – tied more securely this time – another clean-up was required after a blocked drain burst and half-flooded the street.

Dora's street hasn't been alone in meeting with bad luck. Another has had its bunting and Union Jacks stolen –

'vigilance patrols' have since been formed to keep an eye on Bolton's decorations after dark.

Pikes Lane School is also busy with preparations. A big celebration is due to take place at Burnden Park – home to Bolton Wanderers Football Club – involving thousands of the town's schoolchildren. Constance and the rest of Senior II will be taking part in a pageant of Empire. 'We have been practising getting our backs straight for the tableau,' writes one of the girls. Other schools are tasked with singing or maypole dancing, while twelve hundred children will stand in formation to make up the royal initials G. R. VI. The costumes have taken a while to make. 'We are still struggling with the ghastly coronation frocks,' Miss Kemp privately confides.

It was on 7 May, at the end of a week of rehearsals, that Miss Kemp asked her class to write about what they might like to be when they grew up. It was no surprise, perhaps, that royalty was at the front of Constance's thoughts:

> My ambition is to be a very select lady's servant
> like the Duchess of Kent, because I like waiting
> on people and I should see the little newborn
> baby. I should be able to see the dresses they
> wear and if the Queen Mary came I should
> have to wait on her, I'd be delighted if possible
> to see the princesses and the King and Queen.
> My work will be to keep clean the room in
> which they dine, set the table, wash up, and do
> everything about the cookery and at Christmas I
> should buy the babies' toys.

At twelve, Constance already had some of the necessary skills for service. She was proud of knowing 'how to make beds and clean shoes and how to polish furniture and clean windows', learnt by copying her mother. Number 17 Lockbank Street was always spotless – much later, Constance's daughter would associate the smell of Dettol with her grandparents' outside toilet, scrubbed down by her grandma three times a day.

Constance was always well turned out, too. 'Mother is always teaching me different things,' she explained. 'I learn to wash my hair, cut my finger and toenails, I know how to clean my teeth and how to walk properly and talk properly.'

Even so, she knew that royal service would require the highest of standards. 'I should have to train for it,' she realised. 'I could not go without any experience because being a high lady's servant is a great honour. In fact I should have to go to train about three times a week and that would be a lot of money to go to a really experienced woman who knew everything about etiquette.'

Constance's daydreams will change when she meets Charles, a handsome young Welshman from Pontardawe, who is stationed in Bolton with the RAF during the war. They will learn to dance together, and when their second child is born and develops respiratory issues, Charles will take his young family back to Wales to get them away from Bolton's smoke. It is hardly Buckingham Palace, but when they dance every evening together in the Welsh valleys and live out a long, happy marriage it will feel a long way from Bolton, nonetheless.

*

The year 1937 was a critical one for the monarchy. The abdication crisis the previous year had damaged the public image of the Windsors. Royal officials and politicians worried that the new King George VI – shy, reserved and a nervous public speaker – would make a poor contrast to his elder brother, the charismatic and popular Edward VIII, who had stepped down from the throne in order to marry the American divorcee Wallis Simpson. Elizabeth, George VI's wife and the future queen consort, privately told a friend: 'I fully expect that we may be moderately unpopular for some time.' Certainly, Mass Observation's questioning of adults found only lukewarm support for the new king, and considerable disquiet about his leadership qualities.

However, few such anxieties were present among the Pikes Lane girls, for whom the Second World War would see them grow into their adulthood just as it would see George VI grow into his kingship. Later in the summer of 1937, Miss Kemp set them an essay entitled 'The Royal Family', and most of the children were appreciative, loyal and complimentary. 'I think that the royal family do their duty very well and I like them very much,' wrote Joan, while Molly thought that 'the royal family are very nice and that they dress nice too'.

Nor did the girls pay much attention to the former Edward VIII, now the Duke of Windsor, despite the strong loyalties to the former monarch that Mass Observation recorded in other sources. The handful that did include him in their essays were generally of the opinion that he shouldn't have abdicated. 'If I had been Prince of Wales I would have left Mrs Simpson and have been king,' declared one. But most

131

didn't mention the Duke of Windsor at all. Oh, people are 'never bothered' about him and Mrs Simpson, was one girl's dismissive response.

The general absence of the Duke of Windsor from the girls' essays is more surprising as he was the only member of the royal family that most of the girls had ever seen. In November 1932, Edward, then Prince of Wales, had made a rare royal visit to Bolton. Travelling up on the night train from Euston, he was still fast asleep upon arrival and the train was berthed in a siding with passing traffic diverted so as not to disturb him. 'It is understood that he slept soundly,' reported the *Bolton Evening News*, which also informed its readers of the prince's breakfast feast, consisting of grapefruit, porridge, kippers, bacon, sausage, scrambled egg, preserves and dessert.

His carriage passed Pikes Lane later that morning and the children were lined up outside to greet him. The seven- and eight-year olds who would later make up Senior II cheered and waved flags as he passed.

By 1937, a few of the girls have more individual experiences of the royal family or know those who have. Elsie's little sister had been to London 'to see inside the palace for sixpence'. One of the guards had winked at her as she passed – a moment of impropriety that is cheerfully recounted to her teacher by a third sister, Edith.

Edith is a couple of years younger than Elsie – 'age 10½' she writes at the top of her essay, and she is anxious for the Duke of Windsor: Mrs Simpson 'has divorced three husbands. I hope she doesn't divorce him.' She got the number of divorces wrong, but she still had a better understanding than another of her classmates who believed that the king had abdicated because 'the crown was too heavy for his head'.

Mass Observation collected essays from the smaller children at Pikes Lane only occasionally, and this is the only one of Edith's essays that survives. Her daughter thought the topic apt, telling us that Edith continued to be obsessed with the royals throughout her life. Indeed, it fell to Edith's second daughter to live out Constance's fantasies, and she grew up to work for Princess Margaret, first as a dresser and then as a personal assistant. Edith was always eager for titbits.

For most of the girls, knowledge of the royal family is gleaned from the media, and here they find no shortage of information. Amelia points out that 'photos, news and films are heard and seen all over about them . . . There is photos on cups, pence and other things.' 'They are very kind to let the photographer take their photographs and publish them,' writes Jessie.

At school, the year plays out to the rhythms of royal ceremonial. Empire Day is held on 24 May every year, when songs are sung, and special assemblies held to mark the anniversary of the birth of Queen Victoria. Miss Kemp plays her part, as do teachers across the country, but she isn't a fan of the pomp and pageantry. 'One of my kids brought a damned big flag which I stuck in one corner of the room,' she complains.

In the years following the excitement of the Prince of Wales's visit, the girls enjoy extra holidays to celebrate various royal marriages. To mark King George V's Silver Jubilee in 1935, each child at Pikes Lane is presented with a half-pound box of chocolates and a specially designed handkerchief; when he dies a few months later there are prayers and a special service in Saviour's Church.

The children catch black and white glimpses of the monarch at the cinema, where documentaries such as *The House of Windsor* – a half-hour film largely about George VI – play before the main picture. Sometimes such programmes *are* the main picture: in April the girls are taken as a class to the Hippodrome to see *The King's People*, a composition of newsreel shots of British monarchs since Victoria.

And so the girls find it easy to describe the members of the royal household when Miss Kemp asks them to do so: the king is dark and handsome – 'he is also a good Scout'; the queen plumper but finely dressed and smart – 'a good wife and mother'; the queen mother is now old with white hair but still good-looking and tall. Alice opens her essay by declaring: 'I have never seen any of this great family but I think I could well describe them all.'

Each girl can reel off lists of names, marriages and births but, despite their significant knowledge, they are hazier on what the royal family actually do. 'They help us in all ways, they rule the country and stop the people from fighting. I think it is a hard job to rule all the people and to keep them from fighting. They also send soldiers out to war,' writes one. Others understand that the royal role has changed over time and adapted to the growth of democracy: 'Nowadays the king has not as much power as they had in the time of King John, for he is only here to sign laws for the people almost rule themselves.' Nonetheless this girl feels that it is 'the king's duty to rule the country well'.

Royal officials would have been delighted by the girls' support. After the scandal of the abdication, the image of a dutiful king had been promoted by royal aides worried about George VI's unpopularity. A compliant press helped to craft his public image, showing him as a family man who was as committed to his queen and daughters as he was to his country.

The message rubbed off. 'The House of Windsor is a very pleasant and happy family,' said Annie, while Elsie thought 'that they are a very good family and all of them are very devoted to one another. I think that they, being the ruling family, know that it is a very great responsibility and treat it and their subjects with great respect.'

Officials would have been even more thankful to know that not a single girl mentioned the king's stammer.

Of all the Windsors, the girls were particularly drawn to the two princesses. Aged eleven, Princess Elizabeth was only a year or so their junior, while Margaret Rose – in all the essays and without exception, the younger royal is never plain 'Margaret' – was just about to turn seven. The two princesses 'are devoted to one another', wrote Elsie. 'Many children follow their style of dress for they, like their mother, are very nicely dressed. Their hair is dark and they are very pretty. Their manners are exceedingly nice.'

They had strong opinions on the princesses' characters, too, and were convinced of their honour. Amelia explained that 'The princesses are two nice girls, they do not snub the poor ones. They think just as well of the poor ones as they do of the rich ones.' A classmate agreed: 'They are not swanks because they would like to play with anyone if they could do but because of state laws they are not allowed to.'

Several had seen the photographs of the young princesses'

life-size play house and they spoke enviously of Elizabeth's 'very big doll's house which is big enough for her to walk in'.

But any admiration was tempered with a healthy scorn for children who had seen little of the life that the Pikes Lane girls knew. Despite her fascination with the royal household, signs of weakness got short shrift from Constance: 'I think the royal family are very soft indeed because when the King and Queen were giving a garden party at Buckingham Palace just because one of the princesses had a scar on her leg she could not go.' Another girl agreed: 'The children of the royal family get anything they want and therefore they are soft and do not get a good hiding.'

May 12 – Coronation Day – dawns cool and cloudy, and smells of rain. Yesterday, the children had enjoyed a party and concert at school, and each was given a souvenir medal and, as at the last king's silver jubilee, a box of chocolates. Today the schools are closed, as are the mills, and so it is a slow, sleepy start, without the usual clatter of clogs and shouted greetings through the streets.

The ceremony today will be the first time that the BBC and newsreel companies are permitted inside Westminster Abbey for the service, and it will be the first coronation to be broadcast live. Some of the girls listen at home, but cinemas and churches have also set up broadcasting equipment. Later that evening the king will address the nation with his coronation message: 'It is with a very full heart that I speak to you tonight. Never before has a newly crowned king been able to talk to all his peoples in their own homes on the day of his coronation.'

By mid-afternoon the bunting is looking soggy but the mood is cheerful, and women are starting to set out street tables, improvising screens to shelter tables from the weather. A Mass Observer is doing the rounds of Bolton's town centre pubs, which are getting busy. 'Lots of old women wearing red, white and blue hats, singing drunkenly,' he notes.

He stops for a drink in the Roebuck, where a 'very old' woman informs him that 'I'll say long live the king, but I don't know t'bugger.'

'Aye,' says another. 'First they marry then they have a separation and they marry again and you don't know where you are.'

'They be supping cocktails and brandy now,' someone says.

'They can have all their cocks and the tails,' replies the old woman, 'but give me this,' and she points to her beer.

They are all only half-listening to the commentator on the wireless, which is audible from the next room. 'I'll reckon he's knocked back a few pints by now,' a man laughs.

The girls are more likely to be found in their usual haunt of Queen's Park, crowded today with revellers from Bolton and beyond. One girl is there from nearby Westhoughton, and her teacher – Miss Taylor – will later ask her to record her account of the day. She has strong feelings about the band: 'You should have heard the drums banging and the trumpets blowing, it was terrible,' she writes.

The evening pulls in and the coloured lights hung across the streets start to work their magic. Pianos are pulled out or music is provided by banjos, mouth organs and accordions, though the players have different degrees of ability. There are a few rousing bursts of the National Anthem. A Morris dancing troupe is doing the rounds. Almost everyone is wearing paper hats of red, white and blue; some are in full fancy dress. People get rowdier. One girl observes innocently that 'the children are having pop and the grown-ups I don't know what they are having'.

As night starts to fall, Queen's Park looks even less like its usual self. It is buzzing with people now, and there are fairy lights everywhere, even in the water. A silver-clad acrobat dances among the crowds. The sky is glowing orange from bonfires lit elsewhere in the town, and when the fireworks start there are shrieks of delight at the cascades of golden rain and stars of brilliant colour, while some cover their ears against the bangs. Some of the little boys grumble – three men have been employed to set off the display when they would willingly have done the job for free.

Finally, cheers are raised at the gigantic finale, as images of the king and queen are projected in light with messages in coloured fire of 'Long May They Reign' and 'God Save the King'.

In bed that evening, Miss Kemp gives a sigh of relief. She will have sleepy heads in her classroom tomorrow, but she is glad it's over and normal routines can return. The endless preparations had started to get on her nerves. 'How I do loathe red, white and blue,' she tells Mass Observation.

12.

Storm Clouds

A couple of weeks after the coronation a different group of children, hundreds of miles away, are being packed onto a crowded steamship. They are leaving the Basque region of Northern Spain, which is being pounded by the bombs and guns of General Franco's insurgent fascist army, and are being evacuated to Britain.

The British government was initially reluctant to offer a safe haven to the Spanish children and had muttered about promises of non-intervention. A concession has been forced following furious lobbying by charities and activists, given renewed urgency by the details of horrific atrocities that have been filtering through into British newspapers, most recently the saturation bombing of Guernica.

And so nearly four thousand child refugees, accompanied by teachers and priests, arrive in Southampton on May 23. The coronation bunting is still fluttering there, and some of the children wonder if it has been put up for them.

They are sent to a campsite at first – with pilots on the south coast asked to avoid the area for fear of terrifying children who have endured air raids – and then gradually dispersed in smaller groups to refuges around the country. In early June, fifty-four of the children are sent to Watermillock, the nineteenth-century country house just north of Bolton.

Within a day of their arrival, the first Mass Observers come to visit. A small group of girls, aged maybe twelve or thirteen, are sitting on the lawn outside. They are busy appraising some Bolton lads gathered nearby who have been helping prepare the house for its new guests. Chatting away and laughing in Spanish, the girls are making no secret of the subject of their discussions, and the boys are awkward, grinning sheepishly and play-acting back. One is lolloping around 'inanely', aware of their gaze. '¡Este chico está loco!' one of his audience whispers to her friends: 'This lad's crazy!'

One of the Mass Observers is John Martin-Jones, a documentary film-maker tasked with overseeing Mass Observation's cinema research that summer. He speaks decent Spanish, and when the girls realise their comments are understood they become self-conscious in turn and beg him not to translate. He will visit daily and becomes a particular favourite of the children, bringing crayons and drawing books, handing out sweets and taking them for rides on the back of his motorbike. He chides them for calling him 'mister' – call me Martin – and they hang onto his arms and ask for piggy-backs.

Another Mass Observer, Joe Wilcock, has volunteered to help, having previously worked for several years as warden of a hostel for destitute boys in London's East End. Unable to talk to the children, he kicks a ball to them instead. A couple of the girls – the others have now gone in, giggling – return it and they knock it back and forth until Wilcock concedes, exhausted. They play as well as any English schoolboy of the same age, he writes later, with full control, and tricky with it.

Wilcock also writes of his surprise that the children laugh and joke so soon after arrival; he expected them to be more subdued. But later, at bedtime, he sees one girl get out of bed to tuck up another, patting her face and smoothing her hair. He goes downstairs where the doctor is reiterating the need to put sugar in the children's drinks – they are malnourished – and they are interrupted by a scream from upstairs as a child relives her memories in her dreams.

The next day he sits in the kitchen with some children who are helping to wash up. One boy wields a large bread knife. 'This is good to cut the fascists' throats with!' The children become animated, talking over each other about fathers, brothers and uncles who are fighting. One boy imitates an aeroplane dropping bombs, saying, 'Hitler, Franco.' Another pretends to fire a machine gun. A girl of eleven picks up a carving knife and holds it across her throat, making a hissing noise. This is what she would do to Franco, she says.

Over the next few weeks the boys, in particular, become increasingly unruly. They sulk, shout and are rude to the staff. One complains about the food and is told that he should be grateful – his parents are starving in Bilbao. He is traumatised and angry. 'Let them die,' he mutters. When a group of Catholic priests visit, they disapprove of the red flag that some of the children have been flying. They try to take it away, but the children refuse to give it up, and later some of the boys go out and smash one of the headlights of the priests' car. The Spanish teachers struggle to maintain order given their fragile position in the pecking order of the house – like the children, they remain under the authority of the English women in charge.

The English staff are trying their best but don't know how to deal with such behaviour either – nor do most have any experience of supporting children who have been through such terrible experiences. Martin-Jones protests when he is told that five boys are to be caned for their behaviour but is told that a beating is the best way. 'Anyway, I'm running this, and I make the decisions,' the warden tells him.

Nor is he fond of the other punishment used – sending children to the cellar to cool off. It just brings on a frenzied weeping, he writes – though he doesn't discount crocodile tears – and seems to make little difference to their behaviour anyway. He doesn't say whether or not he also worries about the effect of sending war-scarred children to sit alone in a dark, damp cellar (a cellar that, even in the twenty-first century, will still be attracting ghost hunters lured by claims of paranormal activity). The warden herself is distressed when one day she puts a girl in the cellar and then forgets all about her.

As unwelcome news filters through of Franco's victories, the children wonder what might happen to them. One says that if her parents are dead then she'll never return to a fascist Spain – she might run away to Russia instead. 'Well, at any rate, you'll most probably spend our English winter in Bolton,' Martin-Jones tells her, which provokes uproar among the children around him. 'Apparently, the English weather is regarded as a joke that's gone too far,' he explains in his write-up later.

The first children will eventually leave Watermillock only in the following spring, when twenty of the refugees are returned to Spain or to families in exile. Elsewhere across the country, Spanish refugee children are also leaving, although by 1940, with just over four hundred of the original four thousand still in Britain, the difficulties of wartime sea travel will put a stop to further resettlement. By then, many will be reaching young adulthood, and will take their chances with the English weather to settle in Britain for the rest of their lives.

News of the Spanish refugees elicits a range of responses among Bolton residents. There is much curiosity, and numerous visitors 'who just come and stand about the hall, talking and staring, without performing any useful function'. There are regular donations of toys and also of less-useful gifts, including several books 'of the Sunday School variety', which the Spanish children are unable to read. One nine-year-old picks one up and asks Martin-Jones why on earth they are given such things, before taking it away with her. Better a worthless possession than none at all, he thinks.

Meanwhile, fundraising is a constant challenge. The British government has refused to provide financial support for the Basque refugees and insists that money has to be sourced from voluntary and charitable groups. Many in the Mass Observation team are sympathetic and keen to get involved – one of their number, John Sommerfield, has himself recently returned from fighting with the International Brigade in Spain.

Collecting for the Basque children is rolled into existing efforts to raise funds for the dependents of men fallen or fighting in Spain, and in September Mass Observer Zita Baker attends a Spanish Aid meeting. There are about eighty people in the hall, she records, and they look poverty-stricken themselves: 'It was obvious that a meeting to raise money for the audience of this meeting would have been just as profitable.'

She watches as the chairwoman adjusts her expectations. 'Someone has given ten shillings and we would be very pleased to receive another ten to help a mother keep her child and help to fight the war against Fascism in Spain,' she says, to no response. 'We would be glad to receive nine shillings . . . or five . . . or two and six . . .' There is a pause, and a voice says, 'There's a shilling over here.' It is passed across. Nevertheless, when the bowler hat goes around, Baker sees no one decline to add a coin, though she does notice a man in front quietly slip a penny to each of his neighbours so that they too can give.

Doubling up as an excuse for door-knocking, several Mass Observers undertake house-to-house collections and record a range of responses, from the sympathetic ('I wish I could give you a hundred pounds', from a woman who could manage to spare fourpence), to the self-pitying ('I wish somebody would make a collection for me'), to the openly hostile ('These foreigners start these wars, let them get on with it').

They encounter only one person fearful that events in Spain could be a portent of things to come. 'I do hope they don't get our kiddies,' a woman worries as she drops a coin into the tin. 'Joan's only five and Hitler shan't get her, shall he?'

*

The arrival of the Basque children might have been a warning of what war could do, but there were also signs closer to home. In the spring of 1937, shortly before the bombing of Guernica demonstrated the devastating effects of aerial bombing, a call for volunteers to be trained up as air raid wardens had gone out, following the creation of the national Air Raid Wardens Service. By then, Bolton's police force had already begun to drill in anti-gas procedures and was practising the use of respirators, protective clothing and other equipment. The force had the use of a mobile gas chamber loaned out by the Home Office for training.

At the end of 1937, the Air Raid Precautions Act was passed by Parliament, requiring local authorities to make provisions against air attack. Plans were drawn up for the purchase of sirens, and assessments made of the various work hooters that could be used. Three hundred and fifty volunteers had already signed up to be air raid wardens. By September 1939 there would be many times that number, Amelia's stepfather and Mary and Annie's uncles among them.

It was not the first time that civilians had been mobilised to defend against air attack. During the First World War, there had been occasional air raids over Britain conducted first by Zeppelins and then by bombers. By November 1918, 1,413 civilians had been killed by enemy bombing; considerably fewer than the sixty thousand civilian deaths of the Second World War, but terrifying nevertheless for the new horror that it signalled.

The worst raids took place over the capital, where hasty defences were erected and Londoners sought shelter in tube stations just as they would a generation later; in June 1917,

162 people were killed in a daylight raid on the East End, including eighteen children who had been sitting in their infants' classroom on a sunny Wednesday morning until a bomb tore through the roof of their school.

Bolton's only raid of the war came in the early hours of 26 September 1916. The Irwin family – Joseph, Bridget and their five children – had recently moved from 72 Kirk Street to a house a few further down at number 58. Their new house was one of the five destroyed on the street when the German bombs hit, though their old one escaped. Thirteen lives were lost that night, Bridget and her two-year-old daughter Ellen among them.

By 1937 one of the Pikes Lane girls lived at number 72, another of Alice's close friends. We wonder if she ever knew the fate of the family who had lived in the house a generation before her.

The greatest loss of British life during the First World War, of course, had been on the battlefield, and there were few families in the 1930s that weren't haunted by the wartime ghosts of young men. For the Pikes Lane girls, the resting places of uncles they never knew charted the battles of the war: two of Marion's uncles – brothers – killed a fortnight apart at the Somme in 1916; Mary's uncle killed at Cambrai in 1917.

Others returned with damaged bodies. Marion's father had joined up at the beginning of the war like his brothers. Wounded and left overnight in the field, his leg had turned gangrenous and had to be fully amputated. He was discharged in 1917, and by 1939 he was working as a road watchman to supplement his army pension. His false leg – kept in the bedroom and rarely worn – would much later be one of the most vivid childhood memories of his granddaughter, Marion's daughter.

But if children growing up in the 1930s knew that war had rocked their parents, it was not part of their own experience; even some of their fathers had been born too late to fight. The surviving Pikes Lane essays contain no trace of anxiety about the war that was to come. When the girls were asked to imagine their lives after their schooldays, their dreams of becoming hairdressers, shop assistants or teachers were uncomplicated by worries about what else the future might hold.

When Miss Taylor – Miss Kemp's teacher companion in Blackpool – asked her pupils what they would like to be when they grew up, she found that not only did the horrors of war seem distant but that the intervening years had added to a sense of adventure, particularly for the small boys. It is 'frightfully depressing', she wrote, that most of them 'wish to join the Air Force and drop bombs'.

In the week following Armistice Day, 1937, she asked her seven- and eight- year-olds to write down what they'd thought about during the two-minute silence that had been held in the assembly hall. The answers she got back were earnest and innocent: 'Wars are not a bit nice.' But it had also been hard for the children to concentrate on something that had happened so long ago. One boy wrote that he'd 'thought about the soldiers that was in the war. I thought about them who were killed in the war.' Miss Taylor wasn't so sure. 'He laughed all the time, so I don't think this is true,' she clarified in green pencil underneath, for the benefit of Mass Observation.

Of the Pikes Lane girls, Annie's essay describing Heaven

was one of a very few that mentioned war in any kind of context at all. It was neater and better spelt than the essays written by Miss Taylor's younger pupils, but it shared the same conviction that wars were best avoided. 'There is everything in Heaven that you want,' she wrote. 'There are never wars there unless Satan comes along, but then he is always beaten and sent away.'

'Threepenny one, love?' A tall young woman with bright lipstick is holding out a poppy to Zita Baker. 'Yes please,' the Mass Observer replies, searching for the change. There aren't many left in the box, and most of them are the fancier sixpenny silk ones. The seller rummages for the cheaper kind and hands it over.

It is approaching eleven o'clock on Thursday 11 November – Armistice Day – and people are hurrying in the direction of the Cenotaph, the white arch erected in Victoria Square a few years earlier to commemorate Bolton's 3,700 war dead. A Mass Observer had been there a few days earlier for the Sunday ceremony, when a crowd of several hundred gathered to sing 'Abide with Me' and 'Oh God our Help in Ages Past'. On the town hall steps at other end of the square, a man had stood under the red banner of the National Unemployed Workers Movement and shouted to the crowds in a strong Scottish accent of the workers of Spain who had died for a noble ideal, unlike the British people deluded into fighting an imperialistic war.

Several Mass Observers are taking up positions in different locations, recording the rituals of remembrance. There are some Basque children near the Cenotaph. One woman points them out to another: 'There are the Spanish children, bless them, the loves.' 'They look nice, don't they,' her companion replies. 'They've got better coats than my children have got.'

Baker's allocation is Marks and Spencer's, a block away from the Cenotaph. She pops into Woolworths on the way and notes the presence of a cat sitting on the counter with a red poppy pinned to its collar.

Most customers are leaving Marks and Spencer's as she arrives. By five to eleven Baker is the only customer in the shop, and the girls at the various counters are looking at her askance. Then a grey-haired man enters and proceeds to march up and down the aisles. She can't quite catch what he's muttering – just odd words: 'children', 'don't know', 'the people', 'money', 'tonight'. Later she is told that he was at the Battle of Jutland in 1916 and has never recovered from the shellshock.

There's a whistle outside and an alarm goes off in the shop, signalling the hour. Stillness falls immediately. The girls at their various counters bow their heads and some close their eyes. One sobs loudly. She keeps blowing her nose and the sound punctuates the time as it passes. The veteran continues to stride up and down the aisles, declaiming.

Baker can see only three people outside. An elderly woman didn't notice the whistle and is almost kneeling, peering at an object low down in the shop window. Baker watches as the woman suddenly registers the silence. She stands up quickly, embarrassed.

When the second alarm sounds there is immediate activity. The sobbing girl wipes her eyes and turns her face into a smile. The girl at the stocking counter opens up a pile of boxes and starts to remove their contents. Her counterpart at the bag counter gets out her duster. Three of the girls standing at the torch counter chatter and joke.

Within ten minutes the shop is crowded. 'We're not usually this busy on a morning,' one girl tells Baker when she asks. 'Usually people do their shopping in the afternoon but today they've come straight from the Cenotaph.' Baker calls in at Woolworths again as she leaves, which has also filled with customers. Many are crowded around the Christmas card section.

While Baker has been checking out the shops, other Observers are out in the streets. One asks passers-by what they'd thought of during the silence. 'I thought of a couple of pals who were blown to Hell at Ypres,' answers a man with medals pinned to his chest. 'I was also thinking how soon we should be joining up again.'

There is chatter about events in London, where the two-minute silence at the Cenotaph had been briefly disrupted by a protestor – an ex-serviceman – who had shouted accusations of 'hypocrisy' and rushed towards dignitaries before being stopped by police. The following day the press will make much of his status as an escaped inmate of a London psychiatric hospital. 'Likely a communist,' Mass Observation overhears a millworker mutter.

But such sentiments are expressed in Bolton too. Asked what he thinks of Armistice Day, a man mocks the question – 'Go on the dole and they'll tell you,' he says. He is wheeling a handcart with bits and bobs to sell. He's out of work at the moment and sleeping in a doss house. He is a veteran too, but after the war 'they let you go to Hell'. For him, the day had an added sting: 'I always feel bloody miserable on November eleventh; my wife died last year on the tenth.'

Over the following few days several Observers visit the Cenotaph to record the comments heard. 'Don't chrysanths keep a long time'; 'They were somebody's lads, poor things'; 'It's lives not wreaths people should think of'; 'Bolton will have to play hard on Saturday'; 'Aye they will but I think they will win.'

War feels a long way off, but it is going to change the girls' lives.

Left: Constance poses for a portrait. *Photo courtesy of Virginia Powell*

Middle: Constance and her husband, Charles.
Photo courtesy of Virginia Powell

Below: An extract from one of the essays written by Constance, showing her rather touching hopes for her future.

© *Mass Observation*

When I grow up my ambition is to be a very select ladys servant like the Duchess of Kent, because I like waiting on people

A day by the seaside: holiday-makers enjoy the sand and sea air beneath Blackpool Tower. © *Bolton Council*

Above: Annie makes a wise comment in one of her essays. © *Mass Observation*

Middle and *below right*: Some of Blackpool's many amusements, enjoyed by all ages. © *Bolton Council*

Below left: A portrait of Annie taken at the Blackpool weighing machine in 1937. *Photo courtesy of Ann Hill.*

WILKINSON'S SANATORIUM, BOLTON.

On Sunday I went to see my sister at Wilkinson's Sanatorium. (Where) we passed many fields and a lake. The place is situated in the midst of the country and one gets plenty fresh air. The place is very open and is very cold.

The mill chimneys dominate the skyline (*above*), but on the outer edges of the town, places like Wilkinson's Sanatorium (*middle*) try to offer a cleaner environment for the sick. © *Bolton Council*

Below: An excerpt in Mavis's beautiful looping handwriting which describes the Sanatorium's surroundings. © *Mass Observation*

Again, living in a smoky industrial town is brought into sharp contrast when compared with the fresh air of the countryside: Lostock Open Air School (*below*, © *Bolton News*) felt a world away from the tightly-packed terraces where the children lived (*above*, © *Bolton Council*).

Toys are handed out to the
Basque children at Watermillock.

© Hulton Archive/Getty Images

This work is nicer than the mill. In mills you go in clean and tidy and come out like a throng of raggamuffins. But farms are different

Working in the mill could be a tough job, but it was one for which many of the Pikes Lane girls were destined, despite some of their misgivings. Madge contemplates one of the downsides (*above*); work in the cardroom (*middle*) was particularly disliked. The girl pictured (*below*) must only recently have left school. © *Bolton Council*

Left: Nellie, Richard and their father, 1940.

Photo courtesy of Pamela Mortimer and Neil Bannister

Right: Joyce H and Harry, 1944.

Photo courtesy of Lynn Heywood

Left: Mary and her children, shortly after she was widowed in 1951.

Photo courtesy of Sylvia Fenney and Linda Alberts

13.

Heartbreak

Amelia can't quite believe it when the American soldier asks if she'll dance with him. She's a good-looking girl, always prettily dressed. 'She had something about her, a bit of class,' is how her daughter will later remember her. But she's also quiet and shy, and unaccustomed to attention.

Lots of the girls are chasing the Americans, with their drawling accents and Hollywood smiles. They're different to the British men, who are worn down by wartime privation and rationing. Getting herself a GI boyfriend is the sort of stunt Jessie would pull off: Jessie, whose cheeky confidence had given Miss Kemp grief when they were at school; Jessie, who had known, even then, the secrets of how babies were made; Jessie, in whose shadow Amelia often stands, though the two girls are the best of friends.

But Jessie has eyes only for Ernie, who wears the sailor-blue uniform of the Fleet Air Arm; they will be married before the war is over. And it is Amelia to whom the

American soldier is now stretching out his hand. So she takes it.

She has a good time with her American. He has access to luxuries that are hard to get hold of in wartime Britain, and one of his gifts to her is a little powder compact. She works in the mill during the day and sees him in the evening. Often, they join up with Jessie and Ernie and go out dancing. Amelia is a talented singer, too – she will tell her daughter that she sung with Edmundo Ros and his Rumba Band when they performed in Liverpool during the war, although in what capacity has been forgotten.

Then preparations for D–Day get underway and the American troops are moved down to the south coast. Army trucks roll out of Rivington, the little village outside of Bolton where they have been billeted, and the soldiers smile and throw chewing gum and chocolate to the children who wave them off.

And so Amelia never sees her soldier again. He returns to America at the end of the war, and she keeps the powder compact for the rest of her life.

Amelia's childhood had been a sad one. She never knew her birth father, and her mother's marriage to her step-father when Amelia was a toddler brought a cover of respectability. But the little girl was never allowed to forget her illegitimacy, and the birth of a younger sister a year or so later made her feel even more the outsider, though the two girls would grow to be close.

Her stepfather was cold and distant. He was a local Methodist lay preacher and possessed of a 'religious mania', according to the stories later passed down through the family. Both children were taught to fear their God, and when Amelia was asked to write about Hell in a school essay, she showed no hint of the scepticism that appeared in some of her classmates' work. 'Hell is where you go when you are bad. It has a big fire. That is where you are all burned,' she wrote.

Life at home was strict. Asked to write about what she learnt at home, she told Miss Kemp: 'I learn to be in at nine o'clock.' She wasn't always compliant, although she knew that she was meant to be. Reeling off a list of chores she did at home, she added: 'I sometimes say no to something to which I should say yes.'

The worst treatment came from her stepfather's mother who, had she been a different woman, might have loved Amelia as a grandchild. But she couldn't stand the sight of her. She lived only a couple of doors away and was a frequent visitor. Amelia had to be banished to the backyard whenever she came round, lest the old woman refuse to enter the house.

So Amelia learnt how to melt away into the background. At Pikes Lane, she worked studiously (though with more effort than ability) and kept her head down, content to act as a foil to Jessie.

A 'nice child, very quiet' was Cawson's judgement of her when he made his pen sketches of the Senior II girls. 'Must be on front page,' he wrote of Jessie, who was also 'good at sport, great initiative, good at dramatics' and enjoyed 'much freedom at home'.

Life seemed to get no better when Amelia left school. Like most of her classmates, she went straight into the mill, and hated the dirty, noisy, monotonous work.

And then, on 12 October 1941, her house on Punch Street took a direct hit during a German raid. Neither Amelia nor her sister were at home, while their mother was working at the munitions factory, which the bomber might have preferred as a target. Her stepfather had no time – or perhaps no inclination – to get to a shelter. According to family lore, he died on his knees, praying. Two doors down, his mother was also killed.

Amelia's stepfather and his mother were among eleven people to die in the town that night, the deadliest of Bolton's war. Their church grieved for two of the most loyal and dedicated members of its community. 'Duty nobly done', said the death notice in the *Bolton Evening News*.

For Amelia, it felt like a release.

A few years earlier, and Amelia is twelve. She is ready for her midday meal, seated at one of the long tables that run the length of a dining hall: boys on one side; girls on the other. Stew is being served today, with potatoes and peas, and rice pudding to follow. The meal itself looks appetising enough but no one is allowed to start until everyone has been served. The children sit in silence – talking is not permitted either – and wait. There are well over a hundred of them in the room, plus their teachers sitting at the top table, and so by the time she can eat it her food has gone cold.

Amelia is currently attending Lostock Open Air School, a couple of miles to the west of Bolton. The first British open-air school had opened in London in 1907, inspired by experiments on the Continent, and the school at Lostock is one of dozens of similar ones that followed across Britain, pushed by education officials who hailed fresh air and sunshine as therapeutic (and cheap) ways of helping weak, debilitated and malnourished children.

Like many of its counterparts, the Lostock school is deliberately sited out of town, as children sent here are those who are labelled as 'delicate' and judged to be in need of recuperation. The school is set in thirty-three acres of grounds, including a farm that supplies the school with milk, butter, eggs and vegetables. Its bucolic setting feels very far away from Bolton's smoky streets.

Medical examinations take place a couple of times a year at Pikes Lane and Amelia was selected at the last one. She has anaemia, something she will suffer from all her life, and at Lostock she joins children of all ages and from every school in Bolton. They are suffering from malnutrition, debility, bronchitis, asthma or other respiratory conditions. The school is residential, and children go home only at weekends. There are three dormitories for girls and two for boys: at full capacity the school can accommodate two hundred. Later, during the war, one of the girls' dormitories will be used to billet Land Army girls.

We don't know how long Amelia stayed at Lostock Open Air School, but most children are there for at least a term or two. We do know that Amelia will be back at Pikes Lane within a year, in time to write her essays for Miss Kemp to pass on to Mass Observation.

When the children have finished eating, they cross the road to the classroom block. Before lessons resume there is a rest period, with wood and canvas stretchers laid out ready. Some sleep, others doze, a few watch the clouds, listen to the ticking clock and resign themselves to waiting out the hour. One wall of the rest shed is open to the elements; the teachers have been lobbying for years for money to erect a shelter to stop the rain coming in on windy days. It's dry today, but it's extremely cold and there's a hard frost outside even now, in the early afternoon. Amelia can see her breath.

The classrooms are a bit warmer, having been provided with underfloor heating. They are built in an arc, with floor-to-ceiling French windows that are meant to stay open. Today it's cold enough that the teachers will keep their pupils inside, but the furniture is light and moveable. Usually the children carry their desks out into the open air, wearing hats and extra jumpers on top of their serge blue uniforms, if necessary, or wrapping rugs around their legs.

There's an inspector at the school this afternoon, reporting back to Bolton's education committee. It has been five years since his last inspection, in which he criticised the residential matron, a woman 'of advancing years', for 'the certain formality in her outlook'. The same matron is still in charge, and little has changed in this regard, he is sorry to report.

The residential side of the school feels too much like an institution, he says. Save for a few religious pictures in the dormitories, the walls are whitewashed and bare, even prison-like. The uniform is too formal. The food is monotonous: always porridge and milk for breakfast; always bread and butter for tea; the same cycle of midday meals repeated week after week. Tables should be provided in the dining room, he suggests, talking should be permitted, perhaps children should help in the serving of the meal.

He claims that the matron and her attendants treat the children like babies, with no attempt to round off their classroom education with lessons 'in the art of living'. He complains that boys are not given hairbrushes because there is no expectation that they will use them; spoons are provided at mealtimes instead of knives, and as a result many children cannot use cutlery properly.

The inspector once again strongly advises a change of matron ('reorganisation of the staff', he puts it) and acknowledges that the school's institutional feeling might stem from its history. It had opened as an open-air school only in 1928; before that it had been a boys' reformatory for juvenile offenders and, before that, a residential industrial school for destitute children – and therefore, it was assumed, potentially criminal ones. A memory of the time when children were inmates rather than pupils still clings to the building.

But if the spartan living arrangements seem old fashioned to the inspector, Amelia is hardly used to luxury anyway, nor has she any reason to long for the weekend and the warmth of home like some of the other children. Sometimes being here feels special. One of the highlights of the week is a bath – each child has a hot bath once a week – and she loves the feeling of clean hair, a clean body and clean sheets. It gives her a sense of something different.

Nor should the inspector worry that Amelia, at least, is losing out on any training in 'proper behaviour and social conduct'. She will easily catch up with that at home. 'At home I learn to be polite and ladylike,' she will write in one of her Pikes Lane essays the following year. 'I learn to have manners such as to have a knife and fork when I go to anyone's house.'

Many decades later her daughter will read those essays

and laugh. An insistence on table manners – 'that sounds like mum all over', she'll say.

The years immediately following the death of her stepfather were some of the happiest of Amelia's life.

Then the war ended, and she met a young lorry-driver at a dance hall. A hasty marriage was arranged when she discovered that she was pregnant. There was little fanfare and no photos; Amelia did not even wear a wedding dress. She was relieved that at least her own child would not be saddled with the same stigma that she had faced.

She and her new husband had few interests in common; despite the dance hall meeting, he wasn't a dancer and had been dragged there by friends that evening. He didn't like his wife going out. The singing and dancing stopped.

Not that Amelia didn't have more than enough to do at home. Her pregnancy turned out to be twins, and nine more children followed. The house was chaotic and money was always tight. Her husband handed a proportion of his wages over to her for housekeeping but she never seemed to be able to make it stretch. When she had to, she resorted to begging and borrowing extra from friends, afraid to ask for more and fearful of the consequences if he thought she was humiliating him.

The marriage ground her down. 'There was not a lot to her, she never said much,' her daughter told us, remembering that she would sometimes notice her mum with a black eye. But Amelia never said anything, never complained. And it was the children who gave her solace: for them she would do anything.

As a twelve-year-old she had received threepence each

week for minding a neighbour's baby, and the baby appears in the background as she describes the pattern of her days to Miss Kemp. It was another aspect of her essays that her daughter could recognise as she read them in 2020, nearly thirty years after Amelia's death.

She loved all children, and loved looking after children, the same daughter will tell us. Sometimes, if they were quiet, she would nip them gently so that 'then I can love them [till they're] better'. It is hard not to conclude that Amelia was trying to compensate for what she had missed herself.

14.

Shopping

It is late afternoon — 4.30-ish — and a girl about the same age as those in Senior II is strolling arm in arm through town with her mother.

Their first errand is the purchase of a toothbrush, and they disappear into a chemist's shop. Reappearing shortly afterwards, the woman makes to set off again down the street when her daughter tugs at her arm. A booklet in the window has caught her eye: 'Fifty games to play by yourself'. The girl wins the discussion that follows, and a few moments later it has been added to the new red toothbrush in the basket.

Mother and daughter continue up the street, taking their time, the girl pausing to examine the display of dresses in one window, or to covet the set of playing cards in another. A quick stop at the draper's for some buttons, and then to the baker's. 'Not much left, is there?' the woman says, anxiously, looking through the windows. Her daughter pulls a face. 'Wish they'd had those buns again. The ones we saw Friday.' They buy a large loaf and then the pair turn homeward.

The girls of Pikes Lane have been sharing these rituals with their mothers for years. In May 1937, Irene has been helping more than normal – her mum is still working at the mill, though she is seven months' pregnant and can't wait to put her feet up when she gets home at the end of the day. When the baby comes it will be a change for Irene too, and she will have to share both her home and her parents' affections with the new arrival. It is perhaps with this in mind that her mother decides to spoil Irene a little when the holiday for Ascension Day comes around. A mother–daughter afternoon out probably feels like a treat for them both.

The walk into town takes them past some of Bolton's oldest mills, but their trip starts at one of Bolton's most recent attractions, the new milk bar. The first British milk bar opened as recently as August 1935, in London, and yet there are now nearly five hundred nationwide. An Australian invention, though with a very American feel, the bars try to position milk as an exciting, yet healthy, alternative to alcohol. The Milk Marketing Board is, unsurprisingly, an enthusiastic promoter of the trend.

Bolton's milk bar has already created quite a stir. 'Some people seem to come in for the novelty of the place. They ask what there is, not knowing what to order,' an attendant ('a tough, synthetic blonde, about twenty-five') tells a Mass Observer.

The place has bright lighting, bar stools, fake panelling

and huge globes of coloured fruit juices, which are used to add flavouring to the drinks. Milk is on tap, reminding older patrons of the way that beer is served in pubs. But the atmosphere is quite different to that of a backstreet tavern – it is cleanliness and modernity, rather than cosy sociability, that dominates. The women behind the counter wear crisp white jackets and preside over a menu that includes coffee, meat pies and ices – available in wafers, tubs or tall American-style glasses – as well as a plethora of milk-based drinks.

Irene enjoys her milk and, suitably refreshed, she and her mother continue with their shopping, calling in at both Woolworths and Marks and Spencer's in search of dresses. On another occasion, a Mass Observer will write about the women's clothing section of the Marks and Spencer store, describing girls moving back and forth along the rows, looking at the dresses 'rather spasmodically and unsystematically. They feel the material, look at the hems on the short sleeves.' It is terribly crowded as usual, and the Observer doesn't like the crush: 'It is hot and rather smelly, sickly, sweaty.'

For Irene, however, the shopping is a pleasure. By the time she and her mum head back home she is the proud owner of 'some new shoes and two new frocks'.

The Mass Observers were as interested in shopping habits as they were in every other aspect of everyday life, and several of the team spent time following people in and out of the town's many shops. Woolworths was chosen for particularly close surveillance.

Nearly everyone shopped at Woolworths – there were

almost eight hundred British and Irish stores by 1939 – and Bolton was an early adopter. Its branch on Oxford Street was the sixteenth British store to open when it did so in 1912, and a bigger store opened on Deansgate in 1926. When the Blackpool Woolworths opened in 1938 it claimed to be the 'most spectacular' branch in the world, boasting three floors of goods and two restaurants seating four thousand people between them. It drew in vast crowds of holidaymakers, who 'come straight off the train on day excursions and dive into Woolworths for hours at a time'.

Woolworths seemed to sell everything – hardware, haberdashery, toys, food, clothing – and by the late 1930s the brand was well on its way to becoming a cultural icon. It had its own record label – Crown – and shoppers could listen to new releases by artists such as Vera Lynn on the in-store record players. The shop capitalised on the popularity of the cinema with the sale of film magazines such as *Picture Show* and *Picturegoer* for its older shoppers, and Disney-themed merchandise for its younger ones. It also sold sheet music, meaning that girls like Irene – a cinema fan like most of her classmates and able to play the piano a little – could give their favourite film tunes a go at home.

But it was its prices that were Woolworths' real advantage, a theme captured in the songs 'We'll have a Woolworth Wedding' (meaning a cheap one) and 'Nothing over Sixpence', which was quite literally the chain's selling point. The sixpence price ceiling was heavily advertised and captured by Mass Observation's photographer, Humphrey Spender, when he took pictures of a Woolworths window display in September 1937. It meant that those Pikes Lane girls with the smallest amounts of weekly spending money could still find something they could afford: a skein of darning yarn was a penny ha'penny; a quarter pound of nut toffee just threepence.

The popularity of Woolworths was remarked upon even in the Pikes Lane staff room, as a teacher remembered the day trip to Edinburgh made a couple of years earlier by some of the pupils and staff of the senior school. 'When the girls were told this was Princes Street, they just looked,' she told her colleagues. 'When shown the Scott Memorial they just looked. They trailed dully round the War Memorial. But when they were passing Woolworths somebody called out, "Oh look there's Woolworths", and every girl became animated.'

During their time in Bolton, Observers fill hundreds of pages with descriptions that track the movements of customers through Woolworths, recording the precise times spent at each counter, the items bought, and the company kept while doing so. 'Women look at the counter without sharp focus, not so much thinking as waiting for the decision to come,' one concludes.

There's the woman with a small boy of about five, who whimpers all the way round. She buys a quarter of a pound of fruit drops and hands them over to him: 'You're not to eat many of them, see?'

Or the two girls, both about sixteen, who browse the song sheets before moving on to the jewellery counter. One likes the locket containing the picture of Greta Garbo; her friend picks out Robert Taylor and they hold them up to the light to inspect them more closely. The Garbo fan weighs herself on the in-store machine as they leave. The Observer, keen to record every last detail as ever, notes down her weight: seven stones and four pounds.

Mill girls come later in the day, on their way home from work. Three of them are linking arms and pushing their way up the busy aisle, talking and laughing. They cluster around the millinery flowers then double back to the jewellery counter, where they form 'a triangle of heads bent over the trays'. 'I don't know what to get!' one says to her friends. They laugh at her. 'Get a pair of clogs!'

Other observations are more poignant: that of the woman in her mid-twenties – 'poor working class', guesses the Observer, judging by the shabby coat and basket. She hesitates for some minutes outside, deliberating, before going in and heading directly to the sweet counter. She buys a quarter of a pound of broken chocolate cream bars for twopence and goes straight out again. Another woman is looking at brooches and 'takes several in hand. Keeps a white one for a very long time and looks at it with love, holds it with two fingers, tries it on her blouse, puts it back slowly. Leaves.'

It is largely women and girls who are followed, because it is largely women and girls who shop. But men aren't absent from the Observers' accounts. One follows a youngish man wearing a frayed overcoat and muffler: 'Looks unemployed.' He stands for a couple of minutes at the display of colourful artificial flowers, then examines birthday cards. He goes over to the toy counter, where he looks at the dartboards, balls and coloured balloons. Then he leaves, with a glance at the carpentry tools as he passes, putting his collar up against the wind. The Observer makes no further comment, but it's hard not to wonder about the wife and children for whom the man longs to buy a gift.

The Mass Observers are not always successful in their attempts to blend into the background. One, Stella Schofield, has been surreptitiously – she thinks – following two women around the shops for a good half hour when she is challenged.

'Excuse me, but I'd like to know why you are following us? We can't get any shopping done, being followed about like this, I daren't pick anything up. I've lived for thirty-five years and never owed anybody anything yet and I'm being followed about like this as if we had done something wrong.'

Schofield rushes to reassure – she's doing a shopping survey, she explains – and the woman seems mollified. 'We noticed you following us into M&S and Woolworths and then into the Market Hall. If you want to know, I'm looking for a cardigan.'

Another Observer is similarly caught out as he watches and makes notes on two girls in their twenties, probably sisters, discussing lipstick at the make-up counter. One repeatedly catches his eye and, before they leave the shop, she 'stops to do hair in mirror, and to see if Observer following'.

When Miss Kemp asked the Senior II girls about their pocket money, all of them said that they got at least some, usually given by family for help around the house or by neighbours in return for errands or childminding. Most received somewhere between sixpence and a shilling a week. Only a handful were lucky enough to get more; another handful got less. Irene was among the more affluent of the class, earning a shilling from chores done for her parents and grandmother. She told her teacher that she spent threepence of it on trips to the pictures, another threepence on sweets, and then saved the rest for her trips into town.

Nearly all of the girls used some of their money to buy confectionery. Woolworths, with its famous pick and mix selection, was of course a favourite haunt. But there were other places to appease a sweet tooth, and smaller bakers and confectioners, their windows bulging with cakes, tarts and iced buns, also did a good trade among the children (and adults) of the town. Cream cookies were particularly popular with the youngsters, one shopkeeper told Mass Observation: 'These are like tea-cakes with cream in between. Sweet and satisfying, get a lot for a penny.' Another thought their customers' tastes more simple: 'Children like anything with chocolate.'

Some girls were members of the chocolate clubs run by local sweet shops or by individuals for commission. This allowed them to save up for particularly impressive items: perhaps a box of Black Magic, Milk Tray, or even one of the more spectacular club offerings such as a 'Sea Nymph Floating Bowl' filled with Fry's chocolate.

The girls were gifted sweet treats too, and when they wrote about their Easter holidays there were few who forgot to mention chocolate eggs. In fact, March 1937 saw record sales of chocolate in Bolton; a few shopkeepers had run out of stock before the holiday weekend had even begun. Some of the eggs were quite fancy; at least two of the girls received personalised versions with their names written in toffee. One was delighted to receive no fewer than five, plus an egg cup adorned with an image of the king and queen. She generously shared them with her family, only to slightly regret doing so later: 'When I had finished giving them I had only one for myself.'

Madge was one of the few who lost out, commenting on an otherwise happy Easter Sunday that, 'the only thing that was wrong was that there was no Easter egg for me all the others had one'.

Nellie – who usually spends a good chunk of her weekly pocket money on sweets – gets a box of chocolates and 'a large egg' from her mother on Easter Day. The two of them had been to a wedding together the day before and, though she gives few other details, Nellie is keen to describe the food: 'pineapples, jellies, mixed fruits' and 'a large cake with bells, horse shoes, gold shoes and a bride and bridegroom on top'.

Nellie's relationship with her mother will deteriorate as she gets older. She is devoted to her father, and when he has an accident on the railways where he works and then develops Parkinson's disease – the family will always wonder if the two factors were related – she is unhappy with the way her mother treats him. Nellie's own daughter later describes her grandmother in local idiom as a 'creaking gate' – someone always finding something to complain about. 'She was a tyrant!' she tells us.

But from her school essays alone, twelve-year-old Nellie and her mum seem close – and perhaps, at that point, they were. 'My mother sometimes lets me set her hair,' Nellie writes, of a woman who would always be impeccably presented. She describes spending the Ascension Day holiday washing, tidying, dusting and mopping alongside her mum — 'when you dust it makes your hand ache', she writes — before they stop mid-afternoon for a coffee and cake break and then a quick trip to the shops to pick up some bits and bobs. 'At night we stopped in and listened to the wireless,' she concludes. 'Then we had our supper and went to bed.'

When Nellie talks about what she'd like to be when she grows up, she tells Miss Kemp that she'd like to work in a shop. You 'must learn how to keep the shop tidy, to set the window out tidy and to keep your hands clean and your pinafore clean', she writes, reflecting her mother's influence and the domestic training that has been drummed into her. Working in a chemist's shop would be one option, she thinks, 'because it is nice and clean and you learn how to mix medicines for people', but her first preference — this time betraying her sweet tooth — would be to work in a cake shop.

Her choice may well have been fuelled by her delight in chocolate and sweets, but she also knows people in the trade. Her neighbours own a little shop at the end of her street, and she certainly understands what the job involves: 'I like to mop the floors and to make cakes and to sell goods, like toffee, cakes, boiled ham, tongue and other things. You have to learn how to make cakes of different kinds, and to learn how much in weight, and how much they have to pay. Then you have to learn how to give the right money back, and things like that.'

Several of the girls are interested in shopwork, which is one of the fastest-growing occupations of the time and particularly attractive to young women. Those who work for large companies like Woolworths might earn as much as two pounds per week. As one of Nellie's classmates put it, 'You receive a fairly good wage and it is not hard to do the job.'

In fact, the work is demanding, requiring good mental maths, the stamina to stand on your feet all day and a personable way with customers: 'It is most important never to insult a patron or you will lose your post.' But it is clean work, and the working hours are appealing, as another girl explains: 'although you come home late at night you have Wednesday afternoon off. You can go to the pictures at night with your boy or girlfriends.'

The work also offers opportunities for creativity. One shopkeeper tells Mass Observation that she redesigns her own shop window every fortnight, studying her competitors for inspiration and employing tricks she has learnt from the Pitman book of sweet shops. It is another attractive aspect of the job for the girls: Mavis, who also wants to work in a confectioner's shop, particularly relishes the thought of designing the beautiful window displays; as does Joyce D, who imagines being very busy at Easter 'decorating the shop and putting Easter eggs in the window'.

But the girls also know that demand for such jobs is high. 'I think it would be very interesting to get a job that you like, but only a few people do get that sort of a job,' writes Mavis. She's right. She will be working in the mill within a couple of months of leaving school, as will both Nellie and Joyce D.

But Nellie's dream never leaves her. It is close to another twenty years before she manages it, but in the mid–1950s she and her husband Frank start a new life and buy a newsagent's shop in Pendlebury, on the outskirts of Manchester. They will be there for the next twenty-two years.

Despite the trickiness of her relationship with her mother, she inherits many of her ways. Nellie, too, will always be immaculately presented – whether she's at the annual Newsagents' Dinner and Dance, or in her pinny washing out the big bay windows of the shop. And she will be obsessive about cleanliness too, running her finger along the top of a door when she visits her children, checking that it's clean. Right up to her death she'll keep on top of the housework, and will be spotted out in the garden, painting the fences at the age of eighty-eight.

To her own daughter she will pass on her sweet tooth. Nellie's children grow up around the shop and her little girl in particular becomes adept at sneaking chocolate from the shelves. When she leaves to get married, Nellie and Frank will joke that they'll finally be able to make a profit.

15.

Happy Homes

'My number's 8576. I want to win that wardrobe. We've never had one since we've been wed.' A woman is waiting in a long queue outside the Drill Hall on Silverwell Street, chatting to her friend. Up and down the line, others are also talking about the raffle draw. One woman thinks it'll be a fix, the numbers already decided. 'They know. I bet they've written them down,' she says. Another crosses her fingers in the hope that her number will come up. It could happen: 'A friend of mine won seventy-eight pounds for sixpence this year on Littlewoods,' she tells her companion.

It is nearly two o'clock on 22 September 1937 and the fifth annual 'Happy Homes' exhibition, organised by the Bolton Chamber of Trade, is about to open. Like the more famous Ideal Home Exhibition that has been held annually in London since 1908, it showcases the latest innovations in domestic life, and those who visit dream about transforming their homes. By the time the exhibition closes, eleven days later, it will have been seen by thousands.

While they wait to pay the threepence admission, those in the queue – the vast majority of them women – browse the exhibition booklets that are being handed out, in which the organisers claim to have 'combed the country to make this the finest exhibition the provinces have ever seen'.

The booklets also contain the holder's unique raffle number. For each day the exhibition runs, the possessor of a lucky programme will be invited to choose from eight 'magnificent and desirable additions to the home' and be offered it in return for just one shilling. The options include a three-piece Chesterton suite, a wireless set 'in a handsome walnut cabinet, reliable as the Bank of England', and a Hotpoint electric cooker. The coveted wardrobe comes alongside a dressing table and mirrors as part of an oak bedroom suite, normally worth nineteen pounds.

In a separate competition, and offering the most prestigious prize of the event, a new Ford car will be given away to the entrant who comes closest to guessing the exact time at which a mechanical watch will stop. The competition is another fundraiser for the Bolton Royal Infirmary.

Time spent in the queue also offers an opportunity to chat with friends. A Mass Observer overhears a pair of women catching up.

'Harold has only left school this term, and, you know, he's going into the Westminster Bank.'

'That'll be alright, won't it?'

'Yes, the headmaster says it will be a great chance for social advancement.'

Once visitors get inside the building there are distractions aplenty. At stand 49, 'Jokes and Novelties', a salesman is demonstrating a surprise for 'the fellow who comes cadging a cigarette'. He flourishes what looks like a normal cigarette packet: 'The next time he comes . . . you just have this full of water . . . press it as you offer him the packet . . . whoops! Bob's your uncle.'

Elsewhere, a 'Foot Specialist' explains the causes of corns while inspecting a small boy's feet. Madam Lilian, a palm reader from Southport, provides insights into the future as a 'gifted reader of the signs'. For those requiring a different kind of help, Magee's beer is available at stands 78 and 79, promoted with the doubtful claim that 'You cannot keep healthy by better means than a glass of beer'.

Visitors can inspect a selection of aircraft engines and a large model railway ('So, boys, bring your Dad!' suggests the brochure). A huge, 21-foot-long steamship model of the RMS *Queen Mary* sits in a glass case, so that 'you may walk all around to admire the graceful lines of the ship that is the Nation's pride'.

And for an extra threepence, visitors can attend the variety show starring Giovanni, billed as 'the funniest act ever seen in Bolton'. The Mass Observer present doesn't demur, describing the crowd – himself included – as being 'in violent hysterics, almost incapable from laughter', by its end.

But the main focus of the event is home life, and the exhibition space is awash with domestic items of all types, from large electricals, furniture and carpets to toiletries, clocks and fireplaces. Much of the emphasis is upon technologies that will save time, and the names of several products emphasise their labour-saving credentials.

A large crowd gathers around the Easiwork Health Cooker, next to which a Mr E. Elford, 'an acknowledged authority on Health Cookery', is lecturing on food preparation. His company makes the grandiose claim that this new type of pressure cooker is not just a labour-saving gadget but potentially a 'life-saving' one, and the speaker reminds his audience that a good diet can ward off all sorts of illnesses. The crowd is delighted when he hands round samples of its contents for tasting.

Other products also promise to reduce the hard labour of housework and family maintenance. The Bee-Dee Washer offers a wash-day experience without 'back-breaking rubbing and scrubbing and long hours of drudgery at the wash tub'. 'Simply pour hot water into the pan and add soap,' the crowd is instructed. 'Put in the articles to be washed, agitate the handle from side to side for a few minutes, and the clothes are cleaned ready for wringing.' There are appreciative nods from those who know the difficulty of cleaning away the cotton dust that clings to mill workers' clothes.

The most impressive goods on offer at the exhibition are modern and not exactly cheap. Few can afford to buy the most expensive items outright, although credit offers a way of getting goods sooner rather than later. The 'Hotpoint Ladies' are available to discuss hire purchase terms with those tempted by one of the new washing machines; Boardman's of Derby Street offers good rates for the incremental purchase of three-piece suites and bedroom furniture, including part exchange.

But there are also smaller purchases available and a number of people crowd around a stand on which a demonstration of household gadgets such as butter rollers and potato chippers is taking place. Lancaster cloth table coverings are another 'real labour saver – for a wipe with a damp cloth cleans it!'

Even several of the food stands stress their products' time-saving benefits. Smith's Potato Crisps Ltd claim their 'modern table delicacy is becoming an item of daily use in the household, owing to its nutritious value and labour-saving properties'. Elsewhere, jars of liquid chocolate are being touted as revolutionary for the making of cakes and puddings, eliminating the need to grate, heat and melt blocks of chocolate.

Many of those who attend are already familiar with this kind of advertising. The desire for new consumer items has grown across the decade, and popular magazines introduce goods with the promise that they will change lives. Gas fires offer 'the miracle of a clean, labourless home' and the end of a fight against soot and ash; electric cookers 'enable you to cook like a chef!' Electricity is, in fact, 'your servant'. Harpic offers a solution to toilet cleaning that will make 'unpleasant brush work' a thing of the past. Readers are offered help on how to use new products through regular columns such as *Woman's Own*'s 'Hilary Helps with your Housework' with its weekly recommendations about which products to buy.

And, on the whole, the goods at the Happy Homes exhibition draw the approval of visitors who are eager to make their homes more comfortable and their domestic labour less onerous. But they are not a gullible audience. A Mass Observer overhears one visitor exclaim, 'I've had my suite seventeen years. I've never seen such stuff,' to which her companion replies, 'This wouldn't last as long as that, lass.'

We don't know how many of the Pikes Lane girls or their families visit the exhibition, although Dora – who tells Miss Kemp that she'd love to be 'a wardress on the *Queen Mary* and see hundreds of countries' – surely doesn't miss the chance to see the world's largest steamship model of the liner.

There's also a good chance that Irene's mother goes along, with her new baby and Irene in tow. The family have recently moved into a home on Mancroft Avenue, the ring of nearly one hundred and fifty council houses, newly built on the waste ground at the back of Swan Lane Mill. Revelling in the bigger space, the newness and the cleanliness, if Irene's mother did indeed visit the 'Happy Homes' exhibition then she must surely have been tempted by the goods on display.

It's been a few months since Irene wrote about her trip to the shops and milk bar with her mum, and her little sister is now ten weeks old, getting chubby and starting to grab. Recently Irene has been writing in her school essays about helping out by washing the baby's nightdress, vests and frocks, and how her mother 'shows me how to nurse and wash baby's hands and face'. She continues: 'When I have finished my work, I go out and learn how to vault the low railings that go round the small playing field at the front of our house.'

Hundreds of new homes are being built in Bolton every year in the 1930s, of which around one third are funded by the local authority, and Mancroft Avenue is one of a number of such developments. Five thousand new council houses have already been built since the war.

The new houses look different to the town centre terraces. Instead of densely packed two-up, two-down dwellings, the council houses stand back from the road, giving them more space and ventilation. They are bigger: two out of three newly built council houses have three bedrooms. Having a separate kitchen space is welcomed by housewives, while having an indoor bathroom – along with a bath – is appreciated by all the family. Most of the new houses have electricity: in 1920 just seven per cent of British homes had electric wiring compared to more than three quarters in 1938.

It is also rare for a council house to miss out on a garden. When the Bolton corporation produces a 1937 calendar for its tenants, it is illustrated with gardening tips; its annual gardening competitions are designed to encourage tidiness and respectability. When a Mass Observer visits the new Top o' th' Brow housing estate to the north east of the town, he notes 'an unspoken resentment against the man who allows his plot to run to weeds'.

Irene's new house marks a big change from the cramped dwelling that she moves from. She'd spent her earlier childhood years in the tightly packed triangle of streets between Derby Street and Deane Road. Her house had been labelled unfit for habitation and earmarked for clearance earlier in the 1930s.

Within a couple of years, Madge had also made the journey from old to new Bolton when her family moved from their house near Pikes Lane to the Hall i' th' Wood estate.

When asked by Miss Kemp to write about Heaven she had described it as 'a beautiful home'. But she made a point of saying that this heavenly home was quite different to the kind of home she and her classmates lived in – the kind with 'four walls with pictures fixed upon them and a table in the centre of the floor and the sideboard and chairs'.

Madge's description was typical of the Bolton homes that Mass Observation visited. Their investigators made detailed sketches of the way that rooms were laid out and described at length the objects and arrangements within them.

Among the common items of everyday furnishing they also noticed the personal effects that told of past experiences and relationships: the trophies and medals, porcelain ornaments and photographs of men in uniform or couples on their wedding day. There might be a plant at the window, perhaps an aspidistra – satirised by George Orwell as a symbol of 'mingy, lower-middle-class decency' – but also enjoyed by many working-class families as a welcome touch of greenery.

In April, Mass Observer Walter Hood visited a worker's house on Brandwood Street, not so far from Mancroft Avenue, and described its front room in painstaking detail. This particular room had the usual 'well-polished' table at its centre, resting on a square rug. The remaining space was crowded with furniture: leather-bottomed dining chairs; black-and-white spotted easy chairs; a bookcase and a desk; a sideboard; a sewing machine; and a small table with a radio on top.

Every surface was decorated with ornaments or trinkets: wooden candlesticks; a clock; a porcelain Alsatian dog; a blue jug containing four artificial irises; crockery; and two four-inch-high brass peacocks. The mantlepiece – often the focus of a room in the absence of a television – was relatively uncluttered, with the figure of a dancing woman and two glass vases upon it. A small calendar featuring the image of a child was pinned to one wall while a linotype picture depicting an 'Egyptian scene' hung on another.

Many such rooms in houses across Bolton were kept for best only – for guests, or perhaps for Sundays. It was a common tradition in working-class families across Britain, although not everyone thought it sensible. 'It appears that there have been great arguments between husband and wife about which room they should live and eat in,' Hood reported. The wife argues for the back so that 'she can keep the front clean', whereas her husband 'doesn't want the pokey old back room but to enjoy the front'.

In Bolton, the shift from old to new was symbolised by the cleansing of goods as people left the city centre for the more spacious houses further out of town. To ensure that tenants did not inadvertently take vermin or bugs with them to their new lives, the Housing Department advised them to have their furniture, curtains and linen treated in the council's new fumigation station. The process did not always go well.

One resident of the new Johnson Fold council estate wrote a furious report for Mass Observation to put on record a tale of domestic destruction: when his fumigated belongings had arrived at his new address he found damage to his sideboard and kitchen table, his bedding had been scorched a light-brown colour and two eiderdowns 'that cost fifty shillings each' had disappeared. 'There is only one thing that I am pleased about,' he told them. 'And that is that I removed my best suit and the wife's only decent coat.'

Worse still was the experience of sleeping among the newly fumigated items; the family woke in the morning with stinging throats and 'spitting a yellowish slime'. He was outraged that he now owed one pound to the council for the experience, although as a concession to the fact that he was unemployed they told him he could pay it off in instalments of two shillings a week.

Even if the practicalities went smoothly, there were other risks in moving to one of the new council estates. While some enjoyed the drunken sociability of the late bus back from town – 'brilliantly lit, noisily happy, flying over Thicketford Bridge like a bird to its nest' – for others it could feel isolating to move away from family, friends and the haunts they knew, to estates that were often on the edge of the town.

Chapel Street is one of the oldest streets in Bolton – in 1937 already over one hundred years old. Marion knows it well; her mother spent her childhood on this street and her aunt and grown-up cousins still live here, two doors apart from each other.

A crane driver lives at number 9 with his wife and four children. He answers Mass Observation's happiness survey with the reference to home that characterises so many of the responses. 'When a man has done a hard day's work and he comes to a good fire and a good meal, a pleasant wife and happy children. That's what I call happiness.'

A handful of the houses on the street have already been demolished under the slum clearance programme, and so a Mass Observer goes searching for opinions about it, approaching a 'woman about fifty-five, sitting on a chair on the pavement. Silk frock, blue with white flowers.' It's not impossible that the woman is Marion's aunt herself (born in 1887) although with seventy-odd houses on the street, the odds are probably against it.

The woman tells the Observer that 'a lot of fuss is made about slum clearance'. Her house is not so bad, she says, and those who move 'have to pay three shillings, no, four shillings more rent. Who can afford this?'

A neighbour comes across to agree. Her three daughters all work in the mill and are near enough that they can come home for their dinners. If they were out on a council estate, they'd have to get the tram to work, and eat in town. 'It would cost me . . .' she pauses to calculate, 'about one shilling more a week.'

The two women continue to list objections: you wouldn't know anybody; you'd be quite alone; the walls are thin and probably wet too; a bath is alright but you'd have to heat it to use it; the rooms are bigger but how to keep them warm without having to pay for more coal?

They are still shaking their heads and repeating, 'Who can afford it?' when a younger woman passes with a baby in her arms. 'What do you think?' the Observer asks. She's happy to talk, but the little one is grizzly and she needs to get him to bed – will the Observer come too?

Her house is an 'awful hole', the Mass Observer thinks, dirty and very poorly furnished. They go into the kitchen and the woman nods towards a wobbly chair while she fusses with the baby, bending over the cot which sits against one wall.

'I would like to move,' she says, eventually. 'It is so nice up there, there is a garden for the children. And a bath. And I would like to have a nice house. You know I have heard they take all the furniture and disinfect it. You know you can't help it here – you get bugs, they come from all the houses.'

Her story is desperately sad, and they end up sitting for a couple of hours, while the baby sleeps, and she pours out her heart.

'And then I think if my husband would be there away from the bad company perhaps he would stop drinking, if he had a nice garden and the children would be nice and healthier, perhaps he would take to me again. Yes, the money, but it would be better going on the rent than to the pub.'

As for Irene, she is happy with her family's move. She's further away from Pikes Lane and it takes her a good twenty minutes to walk there and back each day, but her aunt still lives near the school, so she has a handy place to stop for a drink or a snack if she feels like it.

Nor has she struggled to make new friends – she never will. Flo, who lives next door, is only a few months younger than Irene. The two girls are soon inseparable. She was my 'Aunty Flo', Irene's son will later tell us.

Mancroft Avenue isn't so different from the old neighbourhood anyway. For all that Bolton is trying to remake itself – a new civic centre is its most ambitious attempt – it is hard to escape the town's industrial character. When Irene stands in her garden, she can see the red brick and dark windows of Swan Lane Mill looming overhead.

16.

Cotton

It's midday and Elsie is on her way to the mill with her elder sister's lunch.

Elsie lives in one of Bolton's new 1930s houses too. It has three bedrooms upstairs and a scrap of garden at both front and back, buffering inhabitants from the street.

But even so, there's never enough space. Elsie is the fourth of eight children – seven sisters and a brother – and since her father was made unemployed he too is around the house much more often than he used to be, his physical presence felt also in his hot temper. He is a veteran of the war and he doesn't like not working, the indignity of being dependent on his three employed children, two of them daughters.

It's her sister Daisy whose meal Elsie is delivering today. Daisy is sixteen, three years older than Elsie, and she's been working at the mill since she left school. She'd left Elsie snuggled under the blankets of their shared bedroom when she'd left for work early that morning – Pikes Lane is closed for a holiday today.

Elsie takes full advantage, and it's mid-morning before she's up and dressed. She helps with her younger sisters and then goes out to play for a while before heading to the mill. 'On my arrival I was taken inside where I watched them at work,' she writes later. 'When they were done we went to see the cardroom, ribbon and derbies, frames and combers. As I have been in many times I know how to work a lot of them. We had a very interesting hour looking around.'

The cotton industry dominated interwar Bolton. In 1937, it employed over thirty thousand men and women across one hundred and twenty mills; more than all of Bolton's other industries combined. Scattered across the town, the mills were a defining presence on the landscape – some of them six or seven storeys high and two or three hundred metres long. Their chimneys cut up the skyline, billowing out smoke onto the slate roofs below.

The smoke cleared only once a year, when the mills shut down for the week's holiday in June. Families and friends would go up onto the hills to look down on their town, enjoying the rare opportunity for a clear view. 'The trees in the parks have black stems,' noticed one Mass Observer, adding that the black came off when rubbed hard with 'a well-spittled finger'. Another visitor was the surrealist artist Julian Trevelyan, who would immortalise the towers, chimneys and smoke of industry in his art.

More than a dozen cotton mills stood within a half-mile radius of Pikes Lane, their towers visible from the playground. Gibraltar Mill was the nearest, within spitting distance. Pikes Lane had stood in its shadow since the building of both school and mill in the early 1870s, the surrounding streets filled every morning with groups of workers about to start their shifts and generations of children arriving for their lessons.

When two Mass Observers visited Swan Lane Mill, the mill which overlooked Irene's house, they were astonished at the feel of the place. As they sat in the small dismal entrance hall, waiting to be shown around, they wondered at the dark, old-fashioned wooden furniture and faded plush seats. The manager's office was hung with heavy green drapes. It had stag heads on the wall and stained glass in its windows. It is what they might have imagined late-Victorian factories to have felt like. The manager and his assistant looked 'absolutely like characters from Dickens', they wrote, wearing wing collars and black alpaca coats. One had a walrus moustache.

And yet Swan Lane was the largest cotton factory in the world at the time, if counted by the number of spindles under one roof. 'Where were the busy, efficient clerks, the smart typists, the important secretaries,' they asked, 'the distant elusive managers, the staff cars parked outside, the telephones, the modern filing-rooms?' They had been expecting shiny-clean efficiency, not this.

But when the girls learnt about the history of cotton at school, part of an educational trend in the 1930s to teach more local history to children, they were told a story of progress, made aware that a century earlier they would already have been in the mill for several years, working long hours in terrible, dangerous conditions, rather than sitting in their comfortable classroom.

The telling of Bolton's past that they heard was infused with local pride: Lancashire innovation had shaped the world; its cotton was supplied to a global market; and the skill of its workpeople was the envy of all. Bolton itself had a particularly special place in the story of cotton as the birthplace of Samuel Crompton, who invented the spinning mule in 1779. His statue stood in the town centre.

It was a version of the story that glossed over the less-palatable aspects of the cotton trade's history: its foundations built on the cheap importation of raw cotton harvested on plantations in the West Indies, and cotton merchants made fantastically wealthy by slavery.

The stories told at school also supplemented and sometimes contradicted what the children already knew. Many came from textile homes, and the vocabulary of the mill peppered their household chatter. It was a foreign language to the uninitiated, one that labelled their family members 'jack frame tenters' (like Elsie's sister), 'twist winders' (Irene's grandmother), 'ring spinners' (Annie's mother), or 'ring frame jobbers' (Constance's father).

Their family connections meant that most of the girls had a good understanding of millwork. They would have had some sense of the journey made by the cotton, which entered the spinning mill in heavy, grimy bales and left the weaving shed as clean, unspoilt cloth, having been carded, combed, drawn, wound, spun, reeled, doubled, bleached, beamed, warped, sized, woven and dyed along the way.

When Elsie enters the mill to find her sister, then, she knows what to expect. She heads straight to the cardroom where Daisy works – a cavernous space containing the dozens of different pieces of machinery that clean and prepare the cotton for spinning.

The heat is the first thing that hits her as she steps inside. Cotton processes demand a warm, damp atmosphere to stop threads drying and snapping. The huge windows that line the walls remain shut at all times: it must never be less than seventy degrees in here but in summer it can top one hundred. The women are working in light cotton dresses to try to keep cool; the younger girls go without stockings. It's thirsty work and they drink a lot of water.

Elsie is soon aware of the dust; by the time she leaves her throat will be dry. Pieces of cotton fill the air, gathering in workers' hair and sticking to sweaty bodies, covering everyone and everything in white fluff so it looks as if they've come in from a snowstorm. Those women with more elaborate hairdos are wearing nets, so they won't have to comb the dust out later and disturb their curls. Most workers will keep a small mirror somewhere about: in her locker, propped on the windowsill or hung on her machine.

And then there is the noise. The cardroom is one of the loudest places in the mill and new girls have to learn to lip-read to have any hope of communicating above the terrific roar of the machines. They call it mee-mawing: the exaggerated movement of mouth and lips to shape the words. Decades later, at least one of the Pikes Lane girls – Annie – will go deaf in her old age, and she'll remember this skill and be glad of it.

Daisy has worked in the cardroom since she started in the mill two years earlier. She began as a setter-on, with the other new fourteen-year-olds. The setters-on assist the card-tenters, the women who attend to the card machines.

Mass Observation is told stories of some tenters who guard their setter-on jealously, sending her out to the toilet or drinking fountain if they think she's about to be poached by another, or even telling her to hide among the skips. 'No, I don't know where she is – haven't seen her for ages,' they'll say.

Daisy had then graduated to card-wiper, with responsibility for keeping the front of the card frames clean. This was a horrible, dirty job, but it meant she got to know the machine, and promotion to card-tenter followed in due course.

Card machines comb the fibres, aligning them so they are ready to be spun. From there Daisy probably moved to the ribbon and derby machines, starting with the odd afternoon covering for someone else off ill, and then given her own machines to look after. From there to combers, then slubbers or boxes, then intermediate or jack frames.

By the time the 1939 register records Daisy, she will be a jack-frame tenter, in charge of the machines that gently twist the bundles of fibre coming from the cards. It's the only job in the room that's paid by piece-rate, giving it a higher status and the potential for better earnings but also increasing the pressure of the work.

When the two Mass Observers visit Swan Lane Mill, they can appreciate the cardroom process as elegant, even beautiful. One describes the cotton in the combing machine as 'twisted over like sharp waterfalls. The spindles looked like rows of milk-bottles,' she writes, 'and when I put my hand on some coils at the top of a cylinder they were silky and rose up and down like a bird'.

But they admit that it surely feels very different to work here. As they continue to move between the rows, the whirling of the machines combined with the roar and the heat makes them feel dizzy. 'It must be dreadful to stay amongst them all day,' they acknowledge, though this does not stop them from professing surprise at the apparent unfriendliness of the workers: 'I thought they looked dismal and colourless, they didn't smile at you unless you smiled very aggressively at them first.' When they arrive back at the office, they are given a clothes brush to clean themselves off.

To work in the cardroom is to hold one of the lower status jobs in the mill; to spend days covered in dirt and fluff. You wouldn't recognise them as the same girls who go out dancing at the weekend, the Mass Observers comment. A supervisor tells them that he often has mothers coming with children and insisting, 'I don't want her to go in the cardroom.'

At midday the frames are stilled, and the workers take a moment to adjust to the change in volume. Daisy welcomes the break. All morning the machines have demanded her full attention and she has had to focus, her eyes moving constantly up and down the line on the lookout for anything wrong. Recent factory legislation requires the provision of foldaway seats and rest benches, but there's rarely time to sit.

She's glad of her sister's company, too. The cardroom is not a sociable place to work. Daisy is isolated between walls of tall machinery, working in among them, and long stretches might pass without sight of another worker. It increases the danger of the work: there have been accidents which have not been discovered for several minutes.

Now the two girls squat on the stone-flagged floor and share sandwiches, brushing off the cotton fibres that settle on their food. Elsie has brought tea and sugar, and they can get hot water from the boiler that's put on for them.

Many of the workers go home in their dinner hour – 'there is a general stampede by almost everyone to get out' – to grab a breath of fresh air, or to get fish and chips, or a pie. Those who stay find quiet corners around the room or go to the small dining room, if they prefer. Many have brought a magazine to read – *Peg's Paper*, *Home Chat*, *Woman and Beauty* – while others chat about a new dress, a keep-fit class, the latest cinema release, or gossip about neighbours. Virtually all the workers in the cardroom are women and there is lots of talk of boyfriends, husbands and would-be lovers.

When they have finished eating, Daisy takes Elsie on a tour of the room. It's only a few days until the coronation and the workers have been decorating their frames, watching each other's efforts with a sense of keen competition. Special occasions are often celebrated in this way, with unofficial 'footings' towards which all workers contribute a few pence, and so foot the bill. Management turn a blind eye so long as no alcohol is brought in. Elsie is impressed: there is a 'host of balloons, flags, balls, photographs and thousands of decorations', she writes in her school essay later.

Elsie goes back home after lunch. She has some chores to do and then spends the afternoon reading. Back at the mill her sister will work until 5.30, watching and waiting for the red bulb in the corner of the room to flash, signalling that the huge engine that powers the mill is about to stop. When it lights up she will be ready to leave, having used idle moments to swap her shoes and put on her coat, all the while still watching her frames, ready for the moment when she and her fellow workers can spill out into the fresher air, relative quiet and easy conversation of the street.

Though she enjoyed visiting, Elsie didn't want to go into the mill like her sister. When she was asked what she'd like to be when she grew up, she wrote of her ambition to be a nurse: 'Since I became a brownie five years ago this has been my aim in life and if possible I still mean to be one.' She was already practising hard. Now a Girl Guide – alongside her best friend Alice – she had a good opportunity to learn first aid. With a multitude of smaller siblings getting into scrapes she also had plenty of willing patients to experiment on.

She had already researched her planned career: she knew she'd have to get something temporary when she left Pikes Lane, as she wouldn't be able to enrol in a training centre until she was eighteen. Once there, though, she was determined to 'put my utmost strength into my work'. She'd have two- or three-years' training, and her duties would initially probably 'be minor ones such as making the patients' beds or washing them'. But she was determined that eventually she could end up as a certified nurse. She'd like to work in a hospital best, but nursing at a private doctor's surgery or even as a district nurse would be better than nothing.

Few of her classmates were keen on the mill as a prospective future either. Annie was another of the girls who wanted to be a shop assistant, because 'inside the shop you are not too hot but in the mill it is stuffy'. Annie's elder sister, like Elsie's, also worked as a card-tenter, and she thought shop work much more appealing.

Madge was put off by the dirt, explaining that 'in mills you go in clean and tidy and come out like a throng of ragamuffins'. She thought it would be nicer to work on a farm, perhaps inspired by her experience with her dad's chickens. 'You don't get as dirty – you go clean and come clean,' she wrote – admittedly a somewhat romantic image of farm life – and 'in the mill you get very hungry and thirsty, but on a farm you don't.'

Jessie was worried about the dirt too: 'When you are working in the mill it makes your mother a great deal of washing, for you have to have two changes of pinafores a week.' She was also anxious about the conditions that left workers vulnerable to asthma and other respiratory problems. Rheumatism was another hazard exacerbated by the daily shift between the warm, damp mill and the outside world. Jessie's mother, another cardroom worker, was frequently unwell and her daughter was scared that the same might happen to her. Office work, Jessie wrote, was 'a clean job and healthy, much healthier than the mill'.

The Pikes Lane children were working-class girls growing up in a northern industrial town recovering from the depression. And yet, despite the seeming inevitability of mill work, they weren't shy to voice an ambition for something better. 'There are quite a few things which flow into my head when a person asks me what I should like to be,' wrote Alice, breezily implying that she could do whatever she chose.

Other girls outlined alternative occupations such as shopwork, hairdressing and teaching, but aimed high here too, hoping that one day they might own shops, run salons, or become headteachers. A girl who wished to be a hairdresser imagined that one day she would manage her own shop, 'and do my own haircutting and if a girl wants to get a job she could come to my shop'.

Another accepted that her probable future lay in the cotton industry but hoped to avoid the worst of the noise and dirt. 'A lot of people do not like going in a mill,' she wrote, but she thought that employment would not be too bad in its warehouse, which was clean and empty of machinery: 'You sit down when you are writing, and you parcel quilts.' Her ambitions were quiet and touching: 'Sometimes if you are getting on very well you learn to answer the telephone.'

But despite all of the girls' reservations, cotton did offer particular opportunities for which children elsewhere might have been grateful. In most parts of Britain, girls who left school at fourteen often entered domestic service before giving up work on marriage. This was usually a low status and poorly paid job, with girls more likely to be working as lonely skivvies in middle-class households than to belong to a large staff in a stately home, rubbing up against the glamour of an aristocratic family. Mill work offered a different kind of life, giving a degree of autonomy and more free time. It offered a limited kind of career progression that could continue beyond marriage but also – much more importantly for these twelve- and thirteen-year-olds – meant no wrench away from their families.

A very different visitor to the mills that year is Penelope Barlow. She is the daughter of the industrialist Sir Thomas

Barlow, a Bolton mill-owner who is also interested in Mass Observation's work and has helped them out with funding. Towards the end of 1937, Penelope adopts the name Phyllis and spends a month working undercover in Musgrave's Atlas Mills, owned by her father, just to the north of Queen's Park.

'Phyllis' spends three weeks in the cardroom before being moved to the winding room for the final week. It's seen as one of the better places to work in the mill. 'You going to winding? It's nice, you'll like it there. It's clean and the money's good,' one of her fellow cardroom workers tells her.

The winding room is much smaller than the cardroom, and not nearly so hot or humid. The machines are still noisy, and it's still hard to have a conversation, but it's 'a rather high-pitched, incessant hum', instead of the deafening roar of the card engines.

The winders prepare the yarn for weaving, winding it from the small cops onto larger cones. There is less variation in employment than in the cardroom. The women replace the cops, remove the cones and pack them up when they're full. They also have to mend the pieces of yarn when they break, achieved by means of a knotter fastened by a strap to the left hand. Barlow struggles with it all morning – 'There is quite an art in getting the thing to make knots at all' – before she gets the hang of it; by the end of the day she will be so used to its feel that she forgets to take it off and will have to creep back to the dark and empty room to return it.

Barlow is put under the wing of Lilian, a twenty-four-year-old winder. After a couple of days, she confesses to Lilian that she will be leaving at the end of the week, that she'd only come 'to get a practical background to a theoretical education and to see how another class of people lived and worked and thought'. Lilian isn't surprised and tells her that 'of course I knew from the first moment that you were not an ordinary new winder, and wondered how long you'd be staying'. Everyone has been guessing, she says.

Lilian is smart and well-read, and eagerly plies Barlow for her thoughts when she recognises her as someone with whom she can share her love of reading. 'Are you a Wells fan too?' she asks, spotting Barlow's book. She has just finished H. G. Wells and Julian Huxley's *Science of Life*, though it took her nine months to get through it. 'Fortunately, I found a friend to lend it to me – I haven't got it, of course, it's too expensive.'

Later, she asks for Barlow's opinions on D. H. Lawrence (because 'he does make you think'), John Galsworthy ('when I read *The Forsyte Saga* I thought it the best book I'd ever read but now I think all the people are too good . . . I do like a bit of real wickedness now and again'), and Bertrand Russell ('I read an article not long ago and I'd like to read something else.').

They chat about other things too, of course. One day, Lilian is knitting, and they talk jumper patterns. Another woman says that she has heard of a school where all the boys are taught knitting – she's seen a photograph of them. The idea tickles Lilian. She splutters into her tea, and it goes everywhere.

Lilian had been ambitious when she was younger, she tells Barlow. When she was at school she won a Shakespeare competition; she had elocution lessons and then she won a Miss England competition in 1933, organised by Bolton's

Palais de Danse but attracting entries from all over the country. She travelled the nation, attending hundreds of public functions and earning 'great praise for the charming and capable way in which she carried out her duties'.

But she hated it and disliked the people she met – 'your class', she tells Barlow. She gave it all up. She's bored again now, she says.

Despite their ambitions, the Pikes Lane girls were always aware that they might be thwarted. As Marion explained, 'I should like to be a dressmaker instead of going in the mill, but people have to go in the mill if there is nothing else.' And, by the time they are recorded in the 1939 register, the mill is where many of them will be found, though Marion will at least manage to secure a coveted spot in the winding room.

Annie will follow her elder sister into the mill and start work as a weaver, though the idea of having a little shop will be a dream that will stay with her all her life; she will tell her children about it. When an elderly woman herself, Annie's daughter will remember going to visit her mum at work; most of all she will remember the noise, the crashing and banging of the machines. Her mother will hate it.

Nor will Irene fulfil her ambition to be a headteacher. She will join her mother in the mill and start work as a ring doffer in the spinning room, a room even less attractive than the cardroom: just as dirty and noisy but with fewer opportunities to progress through different types of job. Later her son, too, will sometimes go to meet her in her dinner hour; they'll sit together and share a meat pie.

Irene will work in several of Bolton's mills, but will be

working at Swan Lane when she finally has to give up work in her early fifties due to a shadow on her lung. When she dies the whole of her floor – fifty women – will come out and pay their respects as her funeral cortège passes.

Elsie, though, gets luckier. Her name is blacked out in the 1939 register, so we don't know what she did immediately after leaving Pikes Lane. But in 1945 she will enrol on a three-year training course in Salford, near Manchester. And in 1948, the year that the new National Health Service comes into being, she will take her place among the first generation of NHS nurses in Bolton Royal Infirmary.

17.

The War

'Hey!' A burly brown-suited man is rushing down the road, in pursuit of three Mass Observers. He is the gaffer on a building site further down the street and the Mass Observers are unaware that they are being chased until he grabs one by the arm and pulls him backwards: 'You're coming with me.' A heated exchange takes place. The Observer wrenches free and threatens to call the police; the stranger says this is exactly what *he* intends to do – he is apprehending enemies of the country.

A crowd is gathering, and a group of women add their voices against the Observers. One says that she has seen them standing about the streets, watching passers-by and quietly making notes – what are they writing about? There are mutters about spies.

Some of the building site workers have also come over to see what's happening, though they seem to find the scene funny. 'Another word from you and I'll knock your head off,' says the brown-suited man as one of the Observers continues to protest angrily. 'I said I would knock assailant's head off first,' writes the Observer later, 'though doubting my capacity to do this.'

After some moments, a repurposed red Coca-Cola lorry draws up and a policeman gets out. He ushers the Observers and their accusers into a nearby air raid warden's shelter. Two detectives join them and ask to see identity cards. They are quickly satisfied, though express surprise that the three young men are all living at the same address. The Observers complain about the rudeness and manners of the informer but are reminded that people are nervous; please don't take any notice.

They leave the warden's post one by one, just in case of trouble, but the women outside pay little attention. They have accosted the policeman again and are telling him about a next-door neighbour who is a Bolshevik and working at the armaments factory. He is promising to investigate.

'The whole incident speaks for the state of the jitters here,' the Observers note later.

It is 29 May 1940, and across the Channel hundreds of thousands of tired and frightened men are waiting on the beaches of Northern France for passage home. It is the third day of the Dunkirk evacuations and the German army continues to press into France and the Low Countries. Nearly fifty thousand soldiers will be brought to safety today, but it is also one of the most dangerous twenty-four hours of the evacuations. Three destroyers will be sunk, taking hundreds of crew and rescued soldiers with them, as U-boats and Luftwaffe bombers wreak destruction.

Back in Bolton the three Observers have been taking opinions on the streets for a few days now. Anxiety is, of course, most acute among those who are waiting for news of loved ones. 'I've got a lad there in France and I don't know where he is,' one man tells them. 'We got a note from him written on the back of a letter we sent him, dated "twenty-third or something". He didn't even know the date. He said he was nowhere making for somewhere and that he would try and drop us postcards as he went along. But we haven't had one yet.'

A lot of people are nervous and admit that the news doesn't look good, even if most are ultimately optimistic. 'It's a mess, isn't it?' says one young woman. 'I think we shall win it all right though.'

Even before they are accosted as spies, the Observers have already been meeting with more resistance than usual in their attempts to elicit opinions from passers-by. 'I'm not saying anything. You want to keep your mouth shut these days,' is the response they get from one woman; 'I thought we were told not to talk,' from another.

Whispers of fifth columnists can be heard everywhere. When France falls at the end of June, the idea that it must have been due to fifth-column activity becomes 'an easy way of explaining things away'. Some Bolton residents find that their nationality makes them suspects; across the country, German and Austrian nationals – 'enemy aliens' – are being rounded up to be interned on the Isle of Man. It doesn't matter that many of them are Jewish and had fled Europe in the 1930s as Nazi persecution began to intensify.

In a fish and chip shop two women are having a conversation about a man they suppose will have been interned.

'He was a fine doctor.'

'Ah, but you don't know. They're all Germans. They ought to intern the lot of them – women and children as well.'

In June, Mussolini throws in his lot with Hitler and Italians join the list of enemies. There are unfounded rumours about Tognarelli, who owns the popular ice-cream shop in the town centre.

Talk of spies bleeds into invasion fears. Later that month the black and yellow signs at the train station are painted over in grey, though the impact is dulled by the fact that the word 'BOLTON' remains to be read in relief. The name of the town is also being painted out on the trams, although again continues to be visible through the thin white paint. 'Possibly this is a first coat,' comments an Observer.

On 13 June, with the Germans about to take Paris, one of the Observers calls in on a family with whom he has become friendly. He finds them huddled in the back room with the kitchen door locked. They are afraid of parachutists, they explain.

A young woman interviewed after the fall of France is more pragmatic and turns the questioning back on the Observer. 'Help me with a problem,' she asks. 'I've got ten shillings and I've got an appointment for a perm tomorrow morning. Shall I spend the money on a perm tomorrow? It doesn't encourage you to spend good money when you think your head might be blown off.' She thinks she might go for a drink that night instead.

By the early summer of 1940, the Mass Observers were winding down their activities in Bolton. Founder Tom

Harrisson had left to go down south in the autumn of 1938 and had been leading Mass Observation's work in London, a.k.a. 'Metrop' to Bolton's 'Worktown'. Research continued, but Bolton was now one of several of Mass Observation's projects, and no longer at its heart.

Their work in the town was temporarily galvanised by the war. Desperate for funds, Mass Observation signed a contract with the government in April 1940 to provide reports on public morale, and for this a northern base was as valuable as a southern one. Mass Observers in Bolton set about counting the number of gas masks carried in public, the frequency of blackout breaches and the amount of attention that people gave to propaganda posters in the streets.

But gradually the focus was shifting, and the last Mass Observers finally moved out of the Davenport Street house in August 1940. Harrisson's study based on Mass Observation's wartime research, *Living through the Blitz*, was published posthumously in 1976, the year after he died in a car accident. It remains one of his best-known books, but there is little about Bolton in it.

The Pikes Lane girls were moving on too. At the end of each term, those who had turned fourteen said goodbye to their classmates and left to join the workplace against a backdrop of mounting international crisis. Alice and Joyce H, two of the oldest in the class, were among the first to leave school in March 1938, the same month that German troops entered Austria and Hitler proclaimed an *Anschluss*.

The next to leave included Amelia, Elsie, Marion and Molly, who all turned fourteen by the summer of 1938, and so were no longer at school that September when German troops occupied the Sudentenland and Neville Chamberlain flew to Munich for crisis talks and came back proclaiming 'peace in our time'.

The youngest children in the group – among them Irene, Joan and Madge – would finish their schooldays in March 1939, as the German army marched into Czechoslovakia. Hitler's next move would be the invasion of Poland that September, which would be the final trigger for Britain to declare war.

The girls entered workplaces readying themselves for a conflict in which success would depend as much upon the factory as the battlefield. Some industries were so critical that its skilled male workers had already been told that they would be exempt from conscription, whether they liked it or not. As a coal miner, Joyce D's father had faced years of unemployment and short-term work in the 1920s and 1930s. It was the war that made him indispensable again, and he worked in the pits for the rest of his life.

Other industries – munitions, armaments, aircraft – expanded and drew on a workforce of women as well as men to do so. In late 1938, a huge purpose-built shell-filling factory opened at Euxton near Chorley, twelve miles north-west of Bolton. This was production on a massive scale, built to accommodate thirty thousand workers drawn from across Lancashire and covering a site of over sixteen square miles. Both Joyce D and Marion worked in munitions during the war, we were told by their daughters. There is a good chance that they were among some of the thousands of women employed here.

Some of Bolton's mills shut down, releasing labour for munitions, but for those that stayed open, work continued more or less as normal, though their big cellars were now converted to air raid shelters and processes shifted to the manufacture of tarpaulin, khaki cloth for uniforms and silk for barrage balloons or parachutes. A Mass Observer spoke to a sixteen-year-old working at a factory producing khaki. 'There was a drawing of Hitler on the conveyor today,' she told him. 'I thought of putting Mr Laurence underneath it (he's one of the bosses) but I didn't dare.'

Annie worked at the mill throughout the war. Later she would tell her children about the fire-watching duties that she had to do during raids, taking her turn on patrol so that an early warning could be raised on any fire started by an incendiary bomb. It was both an exciting and terrifying job for a young teen.

A few of the girls took more unusual employment paths, taking advantage of the new opportunities opening up for women as a result of the war. Madge got a job driving ambulances and jeeps, which she drove without a licence – tests had been suspended during the war. She liked it best when she got to drive an officer around. She never lost her love of vehicles, and after the war she worked on the buses. Later in life she bought a little moped, because she only needed L-plates to drive it. She never did pass her driving test.

In September 1941, Nellie is sixteen and in many ways the war still feels quite distant. Certainly, the town looks different – sandbags have been piled up to protect public buildings and iron railings have been cut down for use in wartime production. There are different faces around, too. The Spanish children have mostly left but have been replaced by fifteen hundred refugees from the Channel

Islands, now under German occupation. Signs in the street point the way to the nearest air raid shelter, though there has been only one bomb as yet, killing two men.

For Nellie, the most threatening sight so far has been the red glow in the sky to the south east, caused by fires burning in Manchester. It had been at its brightest on the two nights of 22–24 December 1940, when the 'Christmas blitz' had destroyed large parts of the nearby city and killed hundreds of people. It is still another month before the deadliest raid of Bolton's war will come, killing Amelia's stepfather and his mother, along with nine others.

And the invasion fears of the previous summer have lost their urgency. Nellie's workplace has formed its own Home Guard branch. Some of them are extremely active – 'a flea couldn't get by them' – but it also includes those who are late to training, or those who arrive drunk. The assessment is provided by Bill Naughton, a local man who had worked for Mass Observation in the past and now can't resist sending a quick update on the state of Bolton's industries, two years into the war. 'I believe this whole munition question merits an intensive investigation. I would be interested in a month's investigation on this aspect alone and feel some hundreds of workers could be interviewed,' he hints, although his suggestion is never taken up, in Bolton at least.

Nellie is working at Dobson and Barlow's factory out at Radcliffe, to the east of Bolton. She walks several miles there and back each day: not so bad in the summer but becoming less attractive now the weather is getting colder and the nights are starting to draw in, made even darker by the blackout. She has plenty of mates to travel with at least

– she is one of eight hundred women among four thousand workers there, most of them from Bolton and many young women like herself.

Dobson and Barlow is one of the oldest textile machinery firms in the world. During the First World War it had temporarily converted to the production of munitions and, since 1935, it has again reinvented itself, adapting its machinery and processes for the manufacture of aircraft wings, as well as pursuing a sideline in shells and bombs.

By the end of the Second World War the firm will have made over six thousand pairs of wings. The men who lead the work here are skilled engineers and proud of their craftsmanship. 'Come and see the jig,' they tell Naughton, referring to the skeletal structure on which the wings are built. 'Tested to one ten-thousandth of an inch. A couple of degrees drop in temperature is enough to throw the measurements out. Right on the bloody dot every time.'

Nellie has a skilled job too, working as a riveter in the wing assembly section. Most women are employed on shell and bomb production, which is less prestigious. They have only recently been allowed to join the men on night shifts, which means bonus pay. 'Workers told me the big incentive is bonus,' reports the Mass Observer, 'and nobody works hard out of a spirit of patriotism.'

There hasn't been much opportunity for that recently, though, and production is currently slack. The workers are blaming a shortage of material and say that a lot of time is wasted waiting for supplies. Naughton talks to some of the men who are employed on painting. He is told that they have been going around 'painting every conceivable spot', while other hands follow superimposing large Vs for

Victory. It is a reminder that war production is not always efficient, even now, two years in.

It seems like a good place to work though, he concludes, and both men and women speak positively of it. They like the concerts given every Wednesday; at lunchtime for day workers and midnight for those on nights. Some of the workers have formed their own brass band. They also like the look of the new canteen that has just opened, although the food itself hasn't as yet lived up to the splendour of the building and there are a lot of complaints about bad quality and high prices. For younger workers like Nellie, working also gives a taste of the independence and friendship that will later be mythologised in the popular memory of women's wartime work.

Not all factories are so well thought of, and the huge shell-filling factory at Euxton – where Marion and Joyce D possibly worked – has a less positive reputation. One disadvantage is the travel, which takes a couple of hours out of most workers' days. Another is the nature of the munition work itself, especially working 'in the powder', which can cause skin disease and jaundice.

But even at Euxton, the young women enjoy the camaraderie and the easy money. One employee – recruited to Euxton from the cardroom of a cotton mill – tells Naughton that she's used to the travelling now. 'We have a drink or two if we go early and the work is very easy. It's not quarter as hard as the cardroom, in the powder. I wouldn't like to do it if I was married, but it is alright now. Especially when you get to know them all.'

He notes that one girl was even 'cashing in' on her 'somewhat golden yellow complexion. She had jet black shiny hair, and her lipstick toned with the general exotic effect; of which she appeared to be rather pleased.'

For their part, the younger men working at the factories are keen on the extra flirting opportunities. At De Havilland's propeller factory, where Molly gets a job, the introduction of more women workers has been popular. 'Nights don't seem as long if you have a few women around,' one man says, and Naughton notes that the employees 'have a reputation for pairing up on Fridays. Husbands who have wives employed at De Havilland try to keep them in on Friday evenings.'

But wartime work is harder for older women who have children or housework to attend to. Nellie hands her wages straight over to her mother at the end of the week, but working housewives have domestic chores and household budgeting to look forward to at the end of a long shift.

Earlier in 1941, several letters had appeared in the local newspaper from women who struggled to get everything done. One woman wrote to say that she didn't get back to Bolton until nearly six o'clock. 'By running all the way I can sometimes manage to get in one shop before closing time,' she explained. 'I find that if it were not for the kindness of neighbours I should, at the end of a day's work, be forced to go home to an empty table.'

Since then, the closing times of shops in the town centre have been extended by half an hour. It helps but doesn't solve the problem. Factory managements still complain that it's hard to get older women to stay on and absenteeism at Euxton is particularly high – about 60 per cent of women never work a full week. 'One can cajole and threaten,' reports a welfare supervisor, 'but women just say that they stayed at home because one of the children was ill, or that they had to do the shopping.'

Frequent recruitment drives have failed to hit their targets, in Bolton as elsewhere. Compulsion will follow in December 1941 as the government's reluctant response to the shortage of volunteers. It will be the first time that British women have ever been conscripted, and the new ruling will require unmarried women between the ages of twenty and thirty and without children to register for work in the Armed Forces, Civil Defence or industry.

In August 1941, in a patriotic attempt to boost recruitment, one of the local newspapers publishes an article describing work for the 'front-line girls' in the filling factory. Many of them feel themselves to be making the weapons for their loved ones in the fighting services, it says. 'It may be that a message goes with a shell destined for a destroyer on the high seas. Or perhaps a filled bullet becomes a love-token to a soldier serving in the East.'

If Nellie reads this and reflects on it when she is at work the next day, the person she will think about most will be her brother. Richard is nearly eight years older than Nellie and they've always been close. He's fiercely protective of his little sister, and she does her best for him, too. 'My brother might have a hole in his stocking and if my mother's busy I mend it,' she'd written in one of her school essays years before.

She misses him desperately. He'd followed his father onto the railways when he left school but is now in the army. For the moment he's safely in barracks somewhere in Britain, along with much of the rest of the army – for

Britain, the war is currently being fought most urgently at sea – but he will see action sooner than most British soldiers and will be among the troops involved in the Italian campaign in 1943. Whenever he comes back on leave, he will bring Nellie little ornaments and other trinkets from the places he passes through.

On one occasion, Nellie is able to send him a message via the Forces' radio station, and he writes to her to tell her of his surprise when he hears the announcer say his name, followed by his sister's 'sweet voice'. He'd been having a drink with his friend – 'lemon squash in case you have any fancy ideas' – and nearly fell off his chair, he tells her.

Later he'll serve in the Netherlands, before returning to Britain in 1945 to take up a quieter job as a railway signalman.

As time goes by, relatives aren't the only men about whom the girls fret. As they grow into young women, they experience their first smuggled kisses under the cover of the blackout. Courtships continue by letter and are bolstered by brief periods of leave. They are all conducted under the threat of loss.

When the girls marry, it's to a generation of men often scarred, in one way or another, by their experiences. Nellie will marry Frank, who served in the RAF and spent time in Iraq, Palestine and Israel. For the rest of his life he will find visiting beaches difficult, though he will enjoy watching his children building different memories of the seaside as they play in the sand.

Irene's future husband is already a soldier when they start courting. He had joined the Territorials in 1938 and so had been deployed early on in the war, including at Dunkirk. Later, he is sent to the Far East and is taken prisoner of war. For eighteen months, Irene won't know if he is alive or dead. When he returns, he will battle nightmares every night. Their son remembers waking up in the dark as a small boy and hearing his dad crying in the next room.

Mary must have worried desperately about her boyfriend Stanley, a young army sergeant. Her mother had been twice bereaved in the First World War, losing her brother at Cambrai in 1917 and then her husband six months later, leaving her with two small children before her second marriage to Mary's father. Mary had grown up knowing of this grief, and is overjoyed when Stanley comes safely home in 1945. But five years later he is called up again to fight in Korea.

Mary will be pregnant with her third child when she hears the news of his death. She will pick herself up from her loss and devote the rest of her days to making the best of things for her children. A second marriage when she is older will give her some company in later years, though she will outlive her second husband too and reach the grand age of ninety. 'Don't grieve for me,' she writes to her children in a letter they find, as she intended, after her death. 'I've had a good life, because of you three.'

Joyce H is luckier than many wartime brides. She meets Harry in the dance hall, where so many of the Pikes Lane girls find their future partners. He volunteers for the Navy and serves on HMS *Aldenham* between 1942–44, undertaking convoy duties around the Mediterranean. In December 1944, the ship hits a mine and goes down in the Adriatic with the loss of one hundred and twenty-six lives. Harry is in Bolton, having been given leave for his wedding day.

The slightly blurred wedding picture is one of the few photographs their daughter has of her parents when they were young: Harry in his sailor's uniform; Joyce with a big bouquet and a dress cut to the knee to accommodate the wartime rationing of material. They will have a long and wonderful marriage.

Epilogue

Chatting to the relatives of 'our' Pikes Lane girls, as we thought of them, was an intense and emotional experience. The girls became mothers in the 1940s and early 1950s, and the men and women we spoke to – their sons and daughters – are mostly grandparents themselves now. It was oddly disconcerting to hear these elderly voices telling us about their mothers, who lived in our minds so vibrantly as living, breathing twelve- and thirteen-year-old girls. It felt the wrong way round, as if the generations had been swapped.

Some of the Pikes Lane girls had passed away decades previously. Madge was the most distant. She had died following a heart attack in 1981, still in her mid-fifties. She had long forgotten her ambition to become a novelist and could never have imagined that one day her words would be published after all. 'She would be so proud,' said her daughter.

Molly had died in 2000 and, by coincidence, we spoke to her daughter a couple of days before the twentieth anniversary of her death. It was Easter, the time of year that her family caught themselves thinking of her most often, reminded by her love of daffodils. Even the grandchildren had known – let's get some daffs for grandma, they'd used to say. Two decades on, they all still miss her desperately.

We sent everyone that we spoke to copies of the essays that their mothers had written in 1937. There were tears, some weren't ashamed to tell us, and they had found it tempting to search the essays for signs of the women that the girls had become. A few said that they could recognise an early form of their mother's handwriting.

Joyce H's daughter and her siblings had known very little of their mother's childhood but told us after reading the essays that 'we understand certain things now'. The places that their mother mentioned in her essay were the same places they had taken their own children, and now took their grandchildren. Such overlap was hardly improbable, of course, but somehow being able to see Joyce's own words on the page strengthened that feeling of connection.

Joyce H was one of the girls who remained most local to the streets in which she'd grown up. She never moved further than a quarter of a mile away from the house where she lived as a child, and was a patient at the doctor's surgery next to Pikes Lane School when she died in 2010. Most of the families we spoke to were still in Bolton or nearby. Constance's daughter told us about her mum in a soft South Wales lilt, but she was one of the few to speak without a Bolton accent.

This was partly, of course, because tracing those contacts still in Bolton was much easier than searching the UK for those who moved away. But it was also because very few of the girls travelled far beyond their home town. We uncovered only a few exceptions. One of the Pikes Lane girls married a local man in 1951, before the newly-weds boarded a ship from Southampton to New York, setting out 'with eight pieces of luggage' for a new life together in the United States. Another – we think – moved to Nigeria in the 1950s with her husband and small son, although returned to Bolton again at some point before her old age. We tried but didn't manage to get in touch.

Even when we did make contact with relatives, the amount of information they could give us varied. Joan was one of the few Pikes Lane girls to remain childless, but she was close to her sister and loved her nephews. We spoke to Steve, who knew much less of his aunt's life than he did of his mother's, but who remembered her very fondly. He had been a professional runner and Joan had often gone along to cheer him on.

Other relatives we spoke to had inherited personal items, photographs and correspondence. Nellie's daughter had all sorts of ephemera from her mother's past, from Sunday school certificates to birthday cards, all things that her mother had so carefully kept. The letter that her brother Richard sent her during the war was among them.

In the end we spoke to the relatives of fourteen of the girls and heard fourteen different stories. But the feeling that we encountered most often was pride. Daughter after son after niece after nephew remembered strong, capable women who'd faced hard times but had – above all – been devoted to their children and brought them up with love, care and attention.

Most of these conversations took place in the early days of the first national lockdown in March 2020. Each call started with a conversation about the surrealness of what was happening and worries about how long it would all last, as we struggled to comprehend what we were living through. Virtual meetings were new to all of us and we grappled with the technology. Most of the time we reverted to phone calls.

By August, when we spoke to Alice's two daughters, the final two relatives we contacted, things were much slicker; Zoom was only too familiar now. Bolton had it tough over the summer, like much of the north west. The town was back in lockdown and they were eager to chat. The two sisters denied inheriting the extent of Alice's talent for dressmaking, though they'd both been busy making masks and scrubs for the NHS.

The enforced time in the house with little else to do, and the prompt that we'd provided by getting in touch, led Margaret, Alice's eldest, to finally get around to looking through the boxes that had been stashed in the loft when her mother had died. It was she who uncovered the photo of some of the Pikes Lane girls in their playground, which is on the cover of this book. Alice is standing on the left, in front of the chalked rectangle.

Alice had also kept some newspaper cuttings relating to her former teacher, Miss Kemp. Alice had been fond of her teacher when she was at Pikes Lane. In his 1937 pen sketch of her, Frank Cawson had added in speech marks (apparently quoting Alice herself) that Miss Kemp 'understands her'.

In autumn 1937, when Pikes Lane was reorganised, Miss Kemp left to join the staff of Castle Hill High School for girls, on the other side of Bolton. There she would teach History for the next thirty-six years, and lead it as headmistress for the final seven, before retirement. She remained a prominent presence in the community, marrying local Labour politician Harry Lucas in 1956, ten years before he became the town's mayor.

The area around her first school, Pikes Lane, looks very different now. Some of the surrounding streets were demolished after the war and the land is occupied by the University of Bolton. The demographic has changed significantly. Today, Pikes Lane Primary School caters for around five hundred children, among whom thirty-two different languages are spoken. The original building has gone, and new premises opened in 2000. Mill towers – now derelict – still break up the skyline, but within a couple of hundred yards there stands a mosque.

But there are continuities too. At its last Ofsted report in 2016, Pikes Lane was classed as 'outstanding'. When we first visited Bolton in 2018, a banner was proudly displayed on the school gates, with a quotation from the report: 'Classrooms are a hive of activity' it proclaimed, 'and burst with ambition'.

Alice goes back to Pikes Lane for the last time in 1975. She and other former pupils have been invited to return as part of the centenary celebrations, to commemorate the opening of the school one hundred years previously.

Alice is in her fifties now. Her two daughters are young women and doing well, and Alice is busy teaching evening classes, passing on her gifts for needlecraft, soft furnishings and embroidery. She is happy, though it's not long before her husband's cancer diagnosis will cast a darker shadow on their lives.

She takes along some of her old school needlework to show the pupils. Her talent had shone even then, and the children who see it are impressed. Later, they're asked to write about their day. One little girl, of Indian heritage, writes her name at the top of a piece of paper and puts down a few lines. 'The thing that caught my eye on the centenary celebration day was the needlework done by Alice,' she writes. 'Alice was a very clever girl. She never made a mistake on the white tablecloth. They took care of their work, they never creased the cloth that they were working on. We just do weaving or cushions and things like that, but they worked harder and harder every day to make things nice and beautiful.'

Somehow the child's essay ends up in Alice's loft. Perhaps the teacher sent it to Alice thinking she might like it; if so, then she was right, for Alice keeps it.

And so it is that, decades later, her daughter sends us a photograph of the child's essay and we come full circle. We read it and wonder if Alice ever thought about what had happened to the essays that she'd written herself at Pikes Lane School, all those years ago.

Acknowledgements

Our first acknowledgement is to the Class of '37; the Pikes Lane girls who we came to know and love and whose school essays are at the heart of this book. Our second is to their families for their generosity in sharing the stories of their relatives' lives. It would have been a lesser book without them. In this regard we would particularly like to thank Linda Alberts, Neil Bannister, Kathleen Birbeck, Kathleen Farrington, Pat Gallagher, Margaret Gallimore, Lynn and Colin Heywood, Ann Hill, Steve Kenyon, Susan Kunce, Margaret R. Marks, David Moran, Barbara Morris, Pamela Mortimer, Brenda Mullineux, J. Olwyn Padidar, Virginia Powell and Dr Alan Rogers. Very sadly, Sylvia Fenney, Mary's eldest daughter, died in August 2020. We are so glad that she got to see her mother's childhood essays, even if she never saw the completed book.

In tracing and contacting relatives we are indebted to Ann Stephenson and her genealogical wizardry. She asked for her fee to go to the charity she volunteers for, the Merton Home Tutoring Service, which provides free English lessons for those in and around Merton, London, who are unable to get to formal classes because of cost, family situation or disability. We were more than delighted to oblige.

Without Mass Observation the girls' essays would never have been kept, and Mass Observation material is reproduced with permission of Curtis Brown Group Ltd, London, on behalf of the Trustees of the Mass Observation Archive. Over numerous projects, it has always been a joy to work with the Archive and its archivists and this one was no exception. The early enthusiasm of Fiona Courage, Curator of the Archive, and Jessica Scantlebury, Senior Archive Assistant, was very welcome and we are also grateful for Jessica's help in contacting the girls' relatives. Both they and Bob Snape, Head of the Centre for Worktown Studies at the University of Bolton, read a draft of the manuscript for us, for which we thank them.

The pandemic meant that we were unable to visit the Bolton History Centre as much as we would have liked, although our earliest visits there were a pleasure. Margaret Calderbank and Brian Whittle won't remember us, but it was with their expert help as volunteers at a Saturday family history drop-in session that we put the first of the girls' names into a genealogical website and realised that we could find out so much more about them.

Gordon Wise, our agent at Curtis Brown, has offered invaluable advice and support throughout. He has helped us to navigate a publishing world that is very different to the academic one that we are more used to writing for. We are extremely thankful to all at Bonnier Books, from Ciara

Lloyd, who first had faith in the project, to Ellie Carr and Justine Taylor who saw it through to completion. They have all been fantastic to work with. We would also like to thank Liane Payne for making such a wonderful map.

Colleagues, friends and family have sustained us throughout, and we are grateful to them all, as well as to Sussex University for supporting this project. Izzy Langhamer, Lucy Robinson and Claudia Siebrecht endured our endless conversations and excitement about the Class of '37. Stephen Brooke, Liz James, Lucy Noakes and Chris Prior acted as generous and critical readers. Cleo Barron read the final draft with a copyeditor's attention to detail, for which we owe her a huge debt. Carol Dyhouse has had a greater influence than she can imagine. Our friend and role model, her intellectual generosity has helped to shape this project from the beginning to the end.

Glyn Prysor acted as a sounding board at every stage and supported us emotionally (Hester with hugs, Claire with coffee). He took on the bulk of Idris's home-schooling when the third national lockdown coincided with the final frenzied weeks of drafting and re-drafting. The book could not have been completed without him.

The writing phase of this project was bookended by two mothers' days. The first, in March 2020, was marked by a deepening of the Covid crisis; by the time the second came around, in 2021, there was tentative hope. Our own mothers were in our minds throughout. We missed them and worried about them, but Audrey Barron and Jan Langhamer, only a generation on from the Pikes Lane girls, were also our inspiration and our motivation. We had always wanted to write something that our mums would love. We are ever so pleased that our dads – Bob Barron and Bill Langhamer – enjoyed reading this book too.

Notes and References

The girls' essays are spread across boxes and folders in the Mass Observation Archive (MOA). Some are in the Topic Collections (TC) at TC 59 4-A (The Royal Family); TC 59 5-D (What I Should Like to be When I Grow Up); TC 59 6-C (Things I Learn at Home that I do not Learn at School); and there is one additional essay – Joyce D's essay on homework – at TC 59 6-B, f. 107. Others are in the Worktown Collection (WC) at WC 49-A (Money, its Use and Importance); WC 49-C (Hell & Heaven); WC 49-D (What I Think of Jesus); and WC 49-E (What I did on my Thursday Holiday & How I Spent my Easter Holiday). On one occasion the girls answered a mixture of questions about their lives – such as their favourite film star, the amount of pocket money they received and how often they went to church – and these are held at TC 59 6-D, while Cawson's pen sketches can be found at TC 59 1-B, ff. 12–17. The Archive also holds essays written by younger children from Pikes Lane as well as children at other local schools. We have used these in Chapter 6 (TC 59 6-C), Chapter 10 (WC 59 A-E), Chapter 11 (TC 59 4-A and TC 59 4-B) and Chapter 12 (TC 59 6-A).

Mass Observation was based in Bolton between 1937 and 1940, and throughout the book we have drawn on the rich material they generated in this period. Mass Observers were fastidious in documenting the tiniest of details and recording overheard conversations verbatim. On the whole the descriptions we use are from 1937, though we have sometimes used their observations from 1938 and 1939 when it helps to conjure up the feeling of the time or particular locations. Mass Observation material is reproduced with permission of Curtis Brown Group Ltd, London, on behalf of the Trustees of the Mass Observation Archive. Copyright is held by the Trustees of the Mass Observation Archive.

Additional material is sourced from publicly available information on Ancestry.co.uk, Findmypast.co.uk and from conversations and correspondence with the girls' relatives. We have used pseudonyms when their families wished us to do so, and for those girls whose relatives we could not trace, despite our best efforts, and who may otherwise be identifiable.

Prologue

For histories of Mass Observation, see David Hall, *Worktown. The Astonishing Story of the Birth of Mass-Observation*, London: Weidenfeld and Nicolson, 2015; James Hinton, *The Mass Observers. A History, 1937–1949*, Oxford: Oxford University Press, 2013; Dorothy Sheridan, David Bloome, & Brian Street, *Writing Ourselves: Mass-Observation and*

Literacy Practices, Cresskill: Hampton Press, 2000. Hinton's book was particularly useful for information on the personal backgrounds of some of the Observers.

Mass Observation's early publications include Charles Madge and Tom Harrisson, *Mass-Observation*, London: Frederick Muller Ltd, 1937; Humphrey Jennings, Charles Madge *et al*, *May the Twelfth: Mass-Observation Day Surveys, An Account of Coronation Day*, London: Faber & Faber, 1937; Madge and Harrisson, *First Year's Work,1937–38*, London: Lindsay Drummond, 1938; and Madge and Harrisson, *Britain by Mass-Observation,* London: Penguin, 1939. Only one of the planned books on Worktown was published: Mass-Observation, *The Pub and the People: A Worktown Study by Mass-Observation*, London: Victor Gollancz Ltd, 1943.
'Write the title "Heaven" and then tell me what you think about it' MOA, WC 49-C, f. 89.

1. Pikes Lane

Mass Observation's notes on schoolchildren can be found at MOA, TC 59 1-B, with material on Pikes Lane specifically at ff. 71–80; Miss Kemp's diary for 10 June 1937 is at TC 59 1-B, ff. 55–70. Further details about the school are drawn from the Board of Education records at The National Archives (TNA), ED 97/779 and ED 16/762, and the Pikes Lane School (senior girls') logbook held at the Bolton Archives and Local Studies Service, SLB/47/23. The latter also includes information about Miss Kemp. Changing ideas about schooling are covered in Laura Tisdall's *A Progressive Education? How Childhood Changed in Mid-Twentieth-Century English and Welsh Schools*, Manchester: Manchester University Press, 2020.

'sermons in brick' Deborah E. B. Weiner, *Architecture and Social Reform in Late-Victorian London,* Manchester: Manchester University Press, 1994, p. 3.

'Lighthouses my boy!' Sir Arthur Conan Doyle, *Sherlock Holmes. The Complete Short Stories*, 'The Adventure of the Naval Treaty', London: John Murray, 1928, p. 515.

'old rambling building' TNA, ED 97/779. Board of Education Interview Memorandum, 15 Dec. 1936.

Pleas for children to come to school in lighter shoes TNA, ED 16/762. Bolton Education Committee Report, 19 Oct. 1936.

'not a place of compulsory instruction but a community of old and young' Board of Education, *Report of the Consultative Committee on the Primary School,* London: HMSO, 1931, p. xvii.

'the curriculum is to be thought of in terms of activity and experience' Board of Education, *Report of the Consultative Committee on the Primary School,* London: HMSO, 1931, p. 93.

2. Expectations

This chapter draws on the Board of Education Inspection Reports of Pikes Lane School that are held by The National Archives at ED 21/32142; we also use material in TNA about the reorganisation of Bolton's schools more generally in the 1930s, especially ED 97/779.

'the residue' TNA, ED 21/32142. Inspector's Report, Pikes Lane School, 17 May 1934.

'A 1934 report of Pikes Lane girls' school had criticised' TNA, ED 21/32142. Inspector's Report, Pikes Lane School, 17 May 1934.

'**the social conditions of the locality . . . admirable manners which the girls have acquired**' TNA, ED 21/32142. Inspectors' Reports, Pikes Lane School, 12 June 1930, 17 May 1934.

'**They all seemed to enjoy this**' MOA, TC59 1-B, ff. 79.

'**solidly built**' TNA, ED 16/762. Bolton Education Committee Report, 19 Oct. 1936.

School leaving report Provided by her family.

3. The Pictures

For a sense of what it was like to go to Bolton's very many cinemas in the 1930s we have used Bolton-born Leslie Halliwell's wonderful *Seats in all Parts. Half a Lifetime at the Movies*, Glasgow: Grafton Books, 1986. Halliwell was born in 1929 and frequented many of the same cinemas, at roughly the same time, as our girls. Two web resources – cinematreasures.org and cinemauk.org.uk – have also provided invaluable information on old Bolton cinemas and other information such as attendance figures. Mass Observation's interviews with Bolton's cinema managers and details of entry prices are at MOA, WC 36-B, along with the description of the Odeon opening at ff. 68–100. The entries to its cinema competition can be found at WC 35-B-E. Mavis's Aunt Bessie's entry is at WC 35-B-C, f. 492. For an overview of Mass Observation's research on the cinema in Bolton and elsewhere, see Jeffrey Richards and Dorothy Sheridan (eds.), *Mass-Observation at the Movies*, London: Routledge & Kegan Paul, 1987; on the cinema more broadly see Jeffrey Richards, *The Age of the Dream Palace. Cinema and Society in 1930s Britain*, London: Routledge & Kegan Paul, 1984.

'the cinema where you meet your friends' Halliwell, p. 112.

'soft plush and worn carpets and Devon violets and sweat' Halliwell, p. 11.

'so far away from the screen that you needed a telescope' Halliwell, p. 118.

'No study of life in an industrial town' MOA, WC 36-A, f. 1.

'factory girls looking like actresses' J. B. Priestley, *English Journey*, London: William Heinemann, 1934, this edition Penguin, 1977, p. 375.

946 million cinema tickets sold https://wwwcinemauk. org.uk/the-industry/facts-and-figures/uk-cinemaadmissions-and-box-office/annual-admissions/ Date accessed: 9 March 2021

'almost like mecca' Halliwell, p. 28.

'small and spiritless' Halliwell, p. 118.

'Ye Olde Pastie Shoppe . . . through the cinema wall' As Halliwell describes on pp. 65–66.

'were practically throwing at everyone who came in' Halliwell, p. 93.

'whose name she scarcely knew but whose caresses spoke the language of love' https://www.youtube.com/watch?v=bQmsJ-x7_G8

'First Lady of the Screen . . . the passionate dreamer and romantic lover' https ://www.youtube.com/watch ?v=IoAgB_sbDOE

a 'faithful' adaptation *Variety*, 31 December 1935. https://variety.com/1935/film/reviews/romeo-and-juliet-2-1200411192/

a Conservative MP cited a survey from Birmingham

House of Commons Debates v. 257, c. 929, Sir Charles Oman, 5 Oct. 1931.

ticket sales peaked at 1.64 billion a year in 1946 https:// www.cinemauk.org.uk/the-industry/facts-and-figures/ uk-cinema-admissions-and-box-office/annual-admissions/ Date accessed: 9 March 2021

4. Making Ends Meet

Our imagining of life on Parkinson Street is influenced by Mass Observation's description of a day on Davenport Street held at MOA, WC 44-F, ff. 1–14. The team lived at 85 Davenport Street during their stay in Bolton. Mass Observation's housing research is at WC 37, including the report of the Bolton Housing Survey at WC 37-A. We have also drawn on material in WC 37-C (especially the Medical Officer of Health's annual report) and WC 37-F (for the interview with Dr Galloway). We found Stephanie Ward's *Unemployment and the State in Britain. The Means Test and Protest in 1930s South Wales and North-East England*, Manchester: Manchester University Press, 2016 and Jim Yelling's article, 'The incidence of slum clearance in England and Wales, 1955-85', *Urban History*, 27:2, 2000: 234–54, to be particularly useful.

Mass Observation had made a study of children's chalk marks MOA, WC 59 1-C.

'if I had one hundred children they would all have to watch all-in-wrestling' MOA, WC 4-4-E, f. 99 and f. 132.

'there should be a bath in every house . . . space for a little garden' MOA, TC 2-3-D, f. 29 and f. 56.

Around seven hundred of the worst houses had been demolished by 1937 MOA, WC 37-C, f. 125

'crawling . . . ready to admit it' David Hall, *Worktown*, p. 128.

'for its poverty, hard living and semi-slum conditions' MOA, WC 23-A, f. 151.

referenced by other former residents in memoirs See for example, Margaret Topliss née Aspinall, 'Down the Pocket', *Bolton Revisited*, https://www.boltonrevisited.org.uk/s-down-the-pocket.html

'happiness is sharing life unselfishly' MOA, TC 7-1-B-1, f. 119.

19 per cent of its working men and 13 per cent of its working women GB Historical GIS / University of Portsmouth, Bolton CB/MB through time | Work and Poverty Statistics | Census Unemployment by Sex, *A Vision of Britain through Time*. URL: http://www.visionofbritain.org.uk/unit/10003179/cube/CENSUS_EMPL Date accessed: 9 March 2021

'the whole *atmosphere* of the place breathed insecurity' Tom Harrisson *et al*, *Britain Revisited*, London: Victor Gollancz Ltd, 1961, p. 33.

'yesterday it was awful . . . one day's holiday in fifteen years' MOA, WC 28-A, f. 2 and 6.

'monies are not freely spent in Bolton, like they are in the south' MOA, WC 30-A, f. 39.

When a Mass Observer visited Bolton's workhouse MOA, WC 27-E, ff. 150–1.

more than two thousand children within the walls A. H. Halsey and Josephine Webb, *Twentieth-Century British Social Trends*, London: Palgrave Macmillan, 2000, p. 531.

'I think everybody is about three weeks from the workhouse' MOA, WC 28-A, f. 5.

5. Church and Chapel

Mass Observation conducted a substantial amount of research on religion in Bolton, intending to write a book on the subject, though they never did. The material is held at MOA, WC 14–26. In particular we used WC 23-A, ff. 150–3 (Pocket Mission); WC 25-A ff. 93–103 (Saviour's Church); WC 16-D (descriptions of the church bells); WC 17-F, ff. 45–52 (Hebron Hall); WC 22-B, ff. 17–27 (Salvation Army); WC 22 E, ff. 118–38 (Saviour's Sunday school); WC 19-D, f. 87–9 (the King's Hall play); WC 19-D, ff. 97–9 (the Victoria Hall concert). We have found Clive Field's work to be particularly helpful especially his 'Religion in Worktown: Anatomy of a Mass-Observation Sub-Project' in *Northern History*, 53:1, 2016: 116–37.

'Sunday is God's gift' MOA, WC 14-E, f. 1.

Bolton is home to forty-one religious denominations Field, 'Religion in Worktown', p. 120.

around forty Anglican churches MOA, WC 15-A, f. 50.

'small but moderately successful' Mass-Observation, *The Pub and the People*, p. 162.

'Smiles are the most common on people's faces' MOA, WC 17-F, f. 129.

'It is a pretty strict place' MOA, WC 1-E, f. 18.

'in the making of sober citizens' MOA, WC 24-A, f. 174.

'hopes everyone will go to bed early' MOA, WC 19-D, f. 78.

'to attract the poorest and the young' MOA, WC 24-A, f. 79.

'a good spell-binder' MOA, WC 20-C, f. 149.

6. Family

Mass Observation's research into household budgets can be found at MOA, WC 32-E, with Walter Hood's account of having tea with a Bolton family at ff. 21–4. Entries to its happiness competition are archived at TC 7. Here we specifically quote TC 7-1-B-2, f. 244 and TC 7-1-B-1, f. 2. We are also indebted to Elizabeth Roberts' *A Woman's Place: An Oral History of Working-Class Women, 1890–1940*, Oxford: Basil Blackwell, 1984.

'Oh look, it's half past four' MOA, TC 59 1-B, f. 68.

blamed for one of the highest rates of maternal mortality in the country MOA, WC 37-F, f. 20.

'unless it's doing my mending, sewing' MOA, WC 32-A, f. 73.

social reformer Margery Spring Rice, Margery Spring Rice, *Working-Class Wives. Their Health and Conditions*, Harmondsworth: Penguin, 1939.

'the whole of Lancashire appeared to be keeping poultry' Priestley, *English Journey*, p. 248.

7. Spare Time

The Mass Observer's visit to the Girl Guide meeting is at MOA, WC 22-F, ff. 13–15 and details about Bolton's Guiding activities are at WC 10-D, ff. 95–104. Material on dancing is in WC 48-C, WC 48-D, and WC 60-D and the carnival observations are at WC 48-B. We have benefitted from Sian Edwards' book, *Youth Movements, Citizenship and the English Countrywide. Creating Good Citizens, 1930–1960*, London: Palgrave Macmillan, 2018, which is very helpful on Girl Guiding, and Liz Oliver's article 'No Hard-Brimmed Hats or Hat-Pins Please': Bolton Women Cotton-workers and the Game of Rounders, 1911–39' in *Oral History* 25:1, 1997: 40–5.

'One, two, three, four, five, six, seven' MOA, TC 41-1-A, f. 190.

'Mrs Mason broke a basin' MOA, WC 49-D, f. 108.

he would far rather watch the town's women play rounders MOA, WC 4-B, ff. 38–9.

'They'll break their bloody necks before long I'll bet' MOA, WC 4-A, f. 54.

'the largest pig in the world' MOA, WC 48-B, ff. 178–80.

8. Sickness

This chapter draws on reports collated by Mass Observation located mostly in MOA, WC 37. This includes *The Annual Report of the Medical Officer of Health* for 1936 and 1937 at WC 37-C and discussions with Dr Galloway, Bolton's Medical Officer for Health at WC 37-F. For the Mass Observers' visits to the different hospitals see WC 37-F, ff. 29–31 and WC 37-G, ff. 34–5 (Isolation hospital); WC 37-G, ff. 29–33 (Townley's X-ray); WC 38-D, ff. 17–27 (Townley's mental health block); WC 37-C, ff. 236–8 (Bolton Royal Infirmary). The reports about the market are at WC 29-C. Also helpful were Janet Greenlees, *When the Air Became Important: A Social History of the New England and Lancashire Textile Industries*, New Brunswick, Rutgers University Press, 2019 and Helen Bynum, *Spitting Blood. The History of Tuberculosis*, Oxford: Oxford University Press, 2012.

'one doubter' MOA, WC 1-E, f. 18.

Fines were usually about twenty shillings MOA, WC 37-F, f. 13.

'**There's many a one as works in a carding-room**'
Elizabeth Gaskell, *North and South*, 1854, this edition
London: J. Murray, 1920, p. 118.

9. Holidays

General observations on holiday preparations, including
rail and bus timetables and numerous Observers' reports
of train and bus stations, can be found at MOA, WC 45-
C, WC 45-D, WC 63-F and TC 58-1-B. Joe Wilcock's
trip to Southport is at WC 45-C, ff. 126–42 and Walter
Hood's trip to Blackpool at WC 45-D, ff. 7–13. Entries
to the holiday competition are at WC 46 with quoted
responses at WC 46-B, f. 21 and f. 170 and WC 46-E, f.
32 and f. 73. Sandra Dawson's article on holidays with pay
was particularly useful: 'Working-class Consumers and the
Campaign for Holidays with Pay', *Twentieth Century British
History*, 18:3, 2007: 277–305.

'**almost literally closes down**' MOA, WC 63-F, f. 5.

'**holiday rainwear**' MOA, WC 45-D, f. 173.

'**men are always dressed in the same damn way**'
MOA, WC 45-D, f. 129.

'**You get Woolworths and Littlewoods there so it's
just the same**' MOA, WC 45-D, f. 138.

'**I asked the bloody gaffer to let me off at half past
four**' MOA, WC 45-C, f. 67.

do you think I was born yesterday, lad? MOA, WC
45-C, ff. 67–8.

He compiles a list of some of the things he sees
MOA, WC 45-C, f. 62.

**fifteen and a half million full-time workers had no
right to a paid holiday** Dawson, p. 292.

'for the first time beautiful in its own right' MOA,
WC 63-G, f. 64.

'the usual strolling girls, many of them in slacks…a
currant bun with his eyes closed' MOA, WC 45-D, f.
178.

'a half-acre muddy boating lake at the edge of the
paddling pool' MOA, WC 61-A, f. 20.

an ice-cream seller at the train station to meet them
MOA, WC 45-C, f. 185.

Have you decided on your holidays this year? MOA,
WC 45-C, ff. 249–50.

10. Blackpool

Mass Observation intended to write a book about Blackpool
and there are drafted chapters of this in the archive at
MOA, WC 60–3, with the raw observational material in
boxes WC 55–9. The book was never completed but it was
published in edited form by Gary Cross as *Worktowners at
Blackpool: Mass-Observation and Popular Leisure in the 1930s*,
London: Routledge, 1990. Specific observations on types
of Blackpool accommodation are at WC 55, including Miss
Taylor's description of where she and Miss Kemp were
staying at WC 55-A, ff. 1–4. Miss Taylor's other observations
are at WC 56-E, ff. 15–18 (at the waxworks), WC 56-F, ff.
1–6 (at the Pleasure Beach), WC 56-H, ff. 3–6 (toilets) WC
58-B, f. 37 (the five-legged cow). Descriptions of Blackpool
beach, with its various stalls and entertainments, are drawn
from WC 61-E and WC 61-F. This chapter also makes use
of Jennie Taylor's article, 'Pennies from Heaven and Earth
in Mass Observation's Blackpool', *Journal of British Studies*,
51, 2012: 132–54. The key texts on Blackpool remain

John Walton's *Blackpool*, Edinburgh: Edinburgh University Press, 1999 and *The Blackpool Landlady. A Social History*, Manchester: Manchester University Press, 1978.

'where the Big Knobs hang out' MOA, WC 60–B, f. 80.

'Of course it makes a difference when you haven't to bother about cooking it' WC 56–F, f. 15.

'these times, arbitrarily fixed and generally enforced by the landladies' WC 60–B, f. 60.

'visitors only pay into them as fines' WC 60–B, f. 38.

'had it out with them' WC 60–B, f. 94.

He reckoned that 95 per cent of Bolton's population had visited Cross, *Worktowners at Blackpool*, p. 19.

One day he set out to survey the myriad palm readers WC 62–F, f. 49.

'The racket, the crowd, the heat, is tremendous' WC 63–A, ff. 86–7.

The country's second underground car park Historic England, Allan Brodie and Matthew Whitfield, *Blackpool's Seaside Heritage*, Swindon: Historic England, 2014, p. 100.

'all the roads suddenly become very straight and wide' Priestley, *English Journey*, p. 249.

'After a running about playing at beach ball' MOA, WC 46–E, f. 58

'Eeeh, I were only eleven eleven last year' MOA, WC 62–B, f. 18.

'And it wouldn't matter if they built a Tower at lots of places' WC 57–C, f. 38.

11. Coronation Day

The *Bolton Evening News* provided details on how Bolton prepared for the 1937 Coronation, and also information about the Duke of Windsor's visit to Bolton in 1932. The decorated street competition is mentioned in the *Manchester Guardian*, 12 May 1937. For details of the Pikes Lane preparations we used the Pikes Lane School (senior girls') logbook held at the Bolton Archives and Local Studies Service, SLB/47/23; Miss Kemp's accounts are at MOA, WC 26-A, ff. 87–91 and TC 59 1-B, ff. 55–70. For descriptions of the day itself we consulted the *Bolton Evening News* and the accounts by Mass Observers including one on Coronation Day in a Bolton pub at MOA, WC 3-B, f. 1. We found Edward Owens' history, *The Family Firm. Monarchy, Mass Media and the British Public, 1932–53*, London: University of London Press, 2019, to be particularly insightful and useful to us in writing the chapter.

'I fully expect that we may be moderately unpopular for some time' Owens, *The Family Firm*, p. 139.

'It is with a very full heart that I speak to you tonight' Owens, *The Family Firm*, p. 185.

12. Storm Clouds

John Martin-Jones' and Joe Wilcock's observations of Basque children at Watermillock can be found at MOA, WC 8-H, while Zita Baker at the fund-raising is at WC 8-G, ff. 9–12 and a report on door-knocking at WC 8-G, ff. 3–5. Bolton's preparations for air raids are detailed at WC 37-B. Observations on Armistice Day are at WC 27-A, including Baker's report at ff. 89–91. On the history of the Basque child refugees in the UK we found the information and resources at https://www.basquechildren.org/ to be invaluable, including an article by Simon Martinez, 'Basque Children in Manchester, Salford and Environs, 1937'. We

also consulted Peter Anderson's article, 'The Struggle over the Evacuation to the United Kingdom and Repatriation of Basque Refugee Children in the Spanish Civil War: Symbols and Souls', *Journal of Contemporary History*, 52:2, 2017: 297–318. On Armistice day we are indebted to Lucy Noakes' article, 'A Broken Silence? Mass Observation, Armistice Day and 'Everyday Life' in Britain, 1937–1941', *Journal of European Studies*, 45:4, 2015: 331–46.
'frightfully depressing' MOA, WC 1-E, f. 153.

13. Heartbreak
Our description of Lostock Open Air School is based on the Board of Education inspection reports of the school held at The National Archives, ED 32/1106. On the history of open-air schools more generally, we were helped by Anne-Marie Châtelet's chapter, 'A Breath of Fresh Air. Open-Air Schools in Europe', in Marta Gutman and Ning de Coninck-Smith (eds.) *Designing Modern Childhoods. History, Space and the Material Culture of Children*, New Brunswick: Rutgers University Press, 2008.
'Duty nobly done' *Bolton Evening News*, 14 October 1941. As cited on the Greater Manchester Blitz Victims webpages at http://www.greatermanchesterblitzvictims.co.uk

14. Shopping
The observations and 'follows' of Bolton's shoppers that we draw on in this chapter can be found at MOA, WC 30-D and WC 30-E. The description of the milk bar is at WC 32-D, f. 1. We also enjoyed consulting the Woolworth Online Museum and this can be found at http://www. woolworthsmuseum.co.uk. On life as a shopgirl see Pamela

Cox and Annabel Hobley, *Shopgirls: The True Story of Life Behind the Counter*, London: Hutchinson, 2014.

'come straight off the train on day excursions' MOA, WC 63-B, f. 41.

'When the girls were told this was Princes Street they just looked' MOA, WC 42-B, ff. 5–6.

'These are like tea-cakes with cream in between' MOA, WC 32-C, f. 1.

'Children like anything with chocolate' MOA, WC 32-C, f. 5.

'Sea Nymph Floating Bowl' MOA, WC 31-A, f. 10.

March 1937 saw record sales of chocolate *Bolton Evening News*, 30 March 1937.

she re-designs her own shop window every fortnight MOA, WC 29-B, f. 165.

15. Happy Homes

Mass Observation's accounts of the 'Happy Homes' exhibition are at MOA, WC 42-J. Its material on Bolton's new housing, including the new estates, is at WC 44-A. This includes Walter Hood's visit to a Bolton home at WC 44-A, ff. 43–64; the complaints about the council's fumigation service at WC 44-A, ff. 32–5; and the discussions on Chapel Street at WC 44-A, ff. 65–6. We have found the following texts to be particularly useful: J. A. Yelling, *Slums and Redevelopment. Policy and practice in England, 1918–45, with particular reference to London*, London: UCL Press, 1992 and Deborah Sugg Ryan, *Ideal Homes, 1918–39: Domestic Design and Domestic Modernism*, Manchester: Manchester University Press, 2018.

'the miracle of a clean, labourless home' *Woman's Own*, 8 Oct. 1938, p. 25.

'enable you to cook like a chef! . . . your servant' *Woman's Own*, 2 May 1936, p. 142.

'unpleasant brush work' *Woman's Own*, 9 May 1936, p. 187.

just seven per cent of British houses had electric wiring Peter Scott and James Walker 'Power to the People: working-class demand for household power in 1930s Britain', *Oxford Economic Papers* 63, 2011: 598–624 at p. 600.

When the Bolton corporation produces a 1937 calendar Bolton at Home, *Quarter Turn*, issue 5, available at the Bolton at Home website, www.boltonathome.org.uk.

'an unspoken resentment against the man' MOA, WC 44-A, f. 10.

'mingy, lower-middle-class decency' George Orwell, *Keep the Aspidistra Flying*, Oxford: Oxford University Press, 2021, p. 21. First published in 1936 by Victor Gollancz Ltd.

'brilliantly lit, noisily happy, flying over Thicketford Bridge' MOA, WC 44-A, ff. 5–6.

'When a man has done a hard day's work' MOA, TC 7-1-B-1, f. 160.

16. Cotton

For Mass Observation's material on millwork and cardroom processes see MOA, WC 40-A-E. The Mass Observers' visit to Swan Lane Mill is at WC 40-E, ff. 13–19 while Penelope Barlow's undercover work is at WC 40-B, ff. 54–170. This chapter also draws on John Walton's *Lancashire. A Social History, 1558–1939*, Manchester: Manchester University Press, 1987.

over thirty thousand men and women across one

hundred and twenty mills MOA, WC 40-A, f. 2; WC 39-A, f. 75.

'The trees in the parks have black stems' MOA, WC 40-A, f. 62.

Swan Lane was the largest cotton factory in the world MOA, WC 39-A, f. 75.

'great praise for the charming and capable way' *Liverpool Echo*, 29 Nov. 1933.

17. The War

In this chapter we draw on observations in Bolton in the early months of the war held at MOA, WC 52. The Mass Observers' reports on being accused of spying are at WC 52-A, ff. 90–7. Reactions to the news from Belgium and France in 1940 are at WC 50-F-H and WC 51-A. Bill Naughton's report on Bolton's wartime industries is in a Mass Observation File Report (FR 856). We have also drawn on Dorothy Sheridan (ed.) *Wartime Women: A Mass Observation Anthology*, London: Mandarin, 1991 and Nobuko Nakamura, 'Women, work and war: industrialisation and mobilisation, Coventry and Bolton, 1940–1946', unpublished PhD thesis, University of Warwick, 1984.

'an easy way of explaining things away' MOA, WC 51-C, f. 207.

Living through the Blitz Tom Harrisson, London: Collins, 1976.

'There was a drawing of Hitler on the conveyor today' MOA, WC 52-A, f. 66.

'By running all the way I can sometimes manage to get in one shop' Nakamura, 'Women, work and war', p. 144, quoting the *Bolton Evening News*, 25 Sept. 1940.

'It may be that a message goes with a shell destined for a destroyer' Nakamura, 'Women, work and war', p. 131 quoting the *Bolton Journal and Guardian*, 25 July 1941.
'lemon squash in case you have any fancy ideas' Richard to Nellie, provided by her family.

Epilogue
'eight pieces of luggage' information from Ancestry. co.uk
five hundred children, among whom thirty-two different languages are spoken
https://www.pikeslaneprimaryschool.co.uk/about-us/what-makes-us-special/